❀ SUFI WISDOM SERIES

VOLUME 1

# PEARLS AND CORAL
## SECRETS OF THE SUFI WAY

BY
SHAYKH MUHAMMAD HISHAM KABBANI

Discourses delivered by permission of his master
Mawlana Shaykh Muhammad Nazim Adil Al-Haqqani,
World Leader of the Most Distinguished
Naqshbandi Sufi Order

December 1991-January 1993
Ann Arbor, Detroit, London, Los Altos, Montreal, New York
City, Oakland, Washington, Woodstock

ISLAMIC SUPREME COUNCIL OF AMERICA

© Copyright 2005 by the Islamic Supreme Council of America.
All rights reserved.
ISBN: 1-930409-07-9
No part of this book may be reproduced, stored in a retrieval system, or transmitted in any form, or by any means, electronic, mechanical, photocopying, or otherwise, without the written permission of the Islamic Supreme Council of America.

Library of Congress Cataloging-in-Publication Data
Kabbani, Shaykh Muhammad Hisham.
    Pearls and coral : secrets of the sufi way : discourses of Shaykh Muhammad Hisham Kabbani delivered by permission of his master Shaykh Muhammad Nazim Adil Al-Haqqani, world leader of the most distinguished Naqshbandi sufi order, December 1991-January 1993, Ann Arbor, Detroit, London, Los Altos, Montreal, New York City, Oakland, Washington, Woodstock.
    p. cm. -- (Sufi wisdom series)
ISBN 1-930409-07-9
1. Naqshabandīyah--Doctrines. 2. Sufism--Doctrines. I. Naqshbandi, Muhammad Nazim
Adil al-Haqqani, 1922- . II. Title. III. Series.
BP189.7.N35K336 2005
297.4--dc22
                                      2005009441

Published and Distributed by:
Islamic Supreme Council of America
17195 Silver Parkway, #201 Fenton, MI 48430
USA
Tel: (888) 278-6624
Fax:(810) 815-0518
Email: staff@islamicsupremecouncil.org
Web: http://www.islamicsupremecouncil.org

Shaykh Muhammad Nazim Adil al-Haqqani (right), world leader of the most distinguished Naqshbandi-Haqqani Sufi Order, with his representative, and author of this book, Shaykh Muhammad Hisham Kabbani.

*From them come forth
the pearls and the coral.*
Holy Qur'an: Ar-Rahman, 55:22

# Table of Contents

| | |
|---|---|
| Publisher's Notes | 9 |
| About the Author | 11 |
| Foreword | 13 |
| The Goal of Saints and Masters | 15 |
|     The Power of Saintly Hearing | 18 |
|     Seclusion | 22 |
|     Gurdjieff's Pursuit of Spiritual Masters | 25 |
| Remember Your Lord | 31 |
|     Underground Idol | 32 |
|     Holding Fire | 33 |
|     Forgive and be Forgiven | 34 |
|     The Unmanned Ship | 36 |
|     The Philosophers and the Child Imam | 38 |
|     God's Servants are Equal | 41 |
| The Cave of Secrets | 43 |
|     Secret of the Prophet's Stay in the Cave | 45 |
|     The Love of Sayyidina Ali | 46 |
|     The Station of the Veracious One | 48 |
|     Arrival in Madinah | 56 |
|     Bayazid Studies with a Shoemaker | 57 |
|     The Spiritual Poles | 59 |
| Advice on Honey | 63 |
| Miracles in the Naqshbandi Way | 64 |
|     Saints are Alive in Their Graves | 66 |
|     Seek a Saint and You Will Find One | 68 |
|     Belief in the Unseen | 71 |
|     Levels in the Naqshbandi Order | 73 |
|     Three Levels of Knowledge | 76 |
| Swimming in Your Orbit | 79 |
|     God Defends His House | 80 |
|     God is not a Torturer | 81 |
|     Saints Move Everywhere | 81 |
|     Use What God Gave You! | 83 |
|     God's Favors: Either Earned or Granted | 84 |
|     Don't Surrender Like a Corpse | 84 |
|     Help Others, for God's Sake | 86 |

| | |
|---|---:|
| **The Necessity for Guidance** | 87 |
| Criteria of the True Guide | 88 |
| Story of Ahmad al-Badawi | 92 |
| Humbleness in Approaching a Guide | 96 |
| **The Ocean of Knowledge in the Heart of Mahdi** | 98 |
| The Six Powers in Every Person's Heart | 98 |
| Deadly Secret | 101 |
| Meaningless Titles and Degrees | 103 |
| Reality is not in Books | 105 |
| **From Love to Annihilation** | 109 |
| Steps to Annihilation | 109 |
| The First Step is Love | 110 |
| Shaykh Nazim's Initiation | 111 |
| Our First Big Test | 113 |
| Lost and Found | 116 |
| A Test of Food | 117 |
| Love Devours Poison | 118 |
| Walk on Nails | 119 |
| **The Anger of the Shaykh** | 120 |
| **Ego and the Pull of Gravity** | 122 |
| Nothing Fills the Eyes but Dust | 123 |
| The Pull of Gravity | 124 |
| Pride: Chief of Negative Manners | 125 |
| **Seeing the Shaykh in the Disciple** | 126 |
| The Shaykh's Representative | 128 |
| The Door of the Shaykh | 129 |
| **The Saint of Rajab** | 131 |
| The Month of God | 131 |
| One Can't Ask God "Why?" | 133 |
| Consider Your Self the Worst | 134 |
| The Secret of the Highwayman | 135 |
| Count the Steps | 137 |
| Hold Anger | 140 |
| What Saints are Expecting | 141 |
| **Submission of the Saints** | 143 |
| The Wrestler and the Shaykh | 143 |
| The Heart-crushing Test | 144 |
| Don't Consider Anything Insignificant | 149 |
| Always Consider Yourself in the Wrong | 150 |
| Everything Comes from the Shaykh | 150 |
| The Final Lesson | 151 |
| Don't Discriminate Between God's Servants | 152 |
| Repay Harm with Mercy | 155 |

| | |
|---|---:|
| The Naqshbandi Golden Chain | 156 |
|     The Unbroken Lineage | 156 |
|     The Water of Life | 158 |
|     Five Levels of the Heart | 160 |
|     The Best Community | 161 |
|     Hadith of the Great Intercession | 161 |
|     Salman, the Persian | 163 |
|     The Prophet's Heart is Washed | 164 |
|     The Forgiven Community | 166 |
|     Sufism is Taste | 168 |
|     A Diamond for a Candy | 168 |
|     Three Levels of Certainty | 169 |
| The Three Lights of Humankind | 173 |
|     The Oceans of Divine Names | 174 |
|     Knowledge of the Naqshbandiyya | 177 |
|     Can God Curse His Creation? | 177 |
|     Angelic Voices | 179 |
|     Have You Heard the Qur'an? | 181 |
|     The Safety of Sham | 182 |
| The Ocean of Shah Naqshband | 185 |
|     The Reason for the Existence of Saints | 186 |
|     The Ocean of Shah Naqshband | 187 |
|     The Farthest Limit | 190 |
|     An Ecstatic Utterance of Bayazid | 192 |
| The Intercession of Saints | 194 |
|     12,000 Oceans of Knowledge on Each Letter of Qur'an | 195 |
|     The Robe of the Prophet and Uwais al-Qarani | 196 |
|     God Did Not Create Humankind for Punishment | 197 |
|     The Dowry of Fatimah | 200 |
|     Islam Honors Ladies | 202 |
| Appendix | 205 |
|     Invocation of Rajab | 205 |
| Endnotes | 207 |

## Publisher's Notes

This book is specifically designed for laypersons and readers unfamiliar with Sufi terms. As such, we have often replaced Arabic terminology with English translations, except in instances where Arabic terms are crucial to the tone and substance of the text. In such instances, we have included transliterations or footnoted explanations.

As the source material is an oral transmission, its language was revised for a written format, and references have been added as appropriate; however, we have tried our best to retain the essence of the author's original talks. We ask the reader's forgiveness for any omissions in this final text.

For those who are familiar with Arabic and Islamic teachings, we apologize for the simplified transliterations. Our experience is that unfamiliar symbols and diacritical marks make for difficult reading by laypersons; as such, please indulge this compromise between accuracy and accessibility.

Qur'anic quotes are centered, highlighted in bold and italics and footnoted, citing chapter name, number and verse. The Holy Traditions of Prophet Muhammad ﷺ (known as *hadith*) are offset, italicized and footnoted referencing the book(s) in which they are cited.

Where gender-specific pronouns such as "he" and "him" are applied in a general sense, it has been solely for the flow of text, and no discrimination is intended towards female readers.

## Universally Recognized Symbols

The following Arabic symbols connote sacredness and are universally recognized by Sufi Muslims:

The symbol ﷻ represents *subhanahu wa taʿala,* a high form of praise reserved for God alone, which is customarily recited after reading or pronouncing the common name Allah, and any of the ninety-nine Islamic Holy Names of God.

The symbol ﷺ represents *sall-allahu ʿalayhi wa sallam* (God's blessings and greetings of peace be upon the Prophet), which is customarily recited after reading or pronouncing the holy name of Prophet Muhammad.

The symbol عليه السلام represents *ʿalayhi 's-salam* (peace be upon him/her), which is customarily recited after reading or pronouncing the sanctified names of prophets, Prophet Muhammad's family members, and the angels.

The symbol ؓ represents *radi-allahu ʿanh/ʿanha* (may God be pleased with him/her), which is customarily recited after reading or pronouncing the holy names of Prophet Muhammad's Companions.

The symbol ق represents *qaddas-allahu sirrah* (may God sanctify his or her secret), which is customarily recited after reading or pronouncing the name of a saint.

# ABOUT THE AUTHOR

Shaykh Muhammad Hisham Kabbani is a world-renowned author and religious scholar. He has devoted his life to the promotion of the traditional Islamic principles of peace, tolerance, love, compassion and brotherhood, while opposing extremism in all its forms. The shaykh is a member of a respected family of traditional Islamic scholars, which includes the former head of the Association of Muslim Scholars of Lebanon and the present Grand Mufti[1] of Lebanon.

In the U.S., Shaykh Kabbani serves as Chairman, Islamic Supreme Council of America; Founder, Naqshbandi Sufi Order of America; Advisor, World Organization for Resource Development and Education; Chairman, As-Sunnah Foundation of America; Chairman, Kamilat Muslim Women's Organization; and, Founder and President, The Muslim Magazine.

Shaykh Kabbani is highly trained, both as a Western scientist and as a classical Islamic scholar. He received a bachelor's degree in chemistry and studied medicine. In addition, he also holds a degree in Islamic Divine Law, and under the tutelage of Shaykh 'Abd Allah Daghestani ق, license to teach, guide and counsel religious students in Islamic spirituality from Shaykh Muhammad Nazim 'Adil al-Qubrusi al-Haqqani an-Naqshbandi ق, the world leader of the Naqshbandi-Haqqani Sufi Order.

His books include: *Keys to the Divine Kingdom* (2005); *Classical Islam and the Naqshbandi Sufi Order* (2004); *The Naqshbandi Sufi*

---

[1] The highest Islamic religious authority in the country.

*Tradition Guidebook* (2004); *The Approach of Armageddon? An Islamic Perspective* (2003); *Encyclopedia of Muhammad's Women Companions and the Traditions They Related* (1998, with Dr. Laleh Bakhtiar); *Encyclopedia of Islamic Doctrine* (7 vols. 1998); Angels Unveiled (1996); *The Naqshbandi Sufi Way* (1995); *Remembrance of God Liturgy of the Sufi Naqshbandi Masters* (1994).

In his long-standing endeavor to promote better understanding of classical Islam, Shaykh Kabbani has hosted two international conferences in the United States, both of which drew scholars from throughout the Muslim world. As a resounding voice for traditional Islam, his counsel is sought by journalists, academics and government leaders.

# Foreword

Our praise and thanks be to God, and our salutations on his beloved Prophet Muhammad and on all sincere servants of the Lord. I am most happy that my son-in-law and deputy, Shaykh Hisham Kabbani has been able to publish this compilation of talks taken from the teachings of our Grandshaykh Mawlana Shaykh 'Abd Allah al-Fa'iz ad-Daghestani ق. May he be granted the best of heavenly rewards.

The teachings of our Grandshaykh are such that those who follow them with attentiveness and diligence may reach perfected stations and attain the stations of the saints in previous times. What has been opened to followers of the Sufi path in this time has never been opened before, regardless of the efforts of the seekers, just as an average citizen today has capabilities at his hands that far surpass those available to even kings in previous centuries. A simple example will illustrate this reality: in the nineteenth century, to go from one end of England to the other would take at least two days by locomotive. Today, airline passengers travel at twice the speed of sound in Concorde jets, crossing all of England in a few short minutes.

As the world around us darkens with negativity, many seek the beacon of light that will lead them to the Divine shelter of peace and protection. We therefore sought to present the spiritual discipline dating back to Prophet Muhammad ﷺ in the early seventh century, preserved by the Naqshbandi Sufi Masters over the course of forty generations. These lessons are designed to overcome doubt and other negative attributes that bind one to the physical world, thereby opening the heart to spiritual elevation.

These talks are alive with the tales of spiritual masters of the Sufi path, and in the retelling of their spiritual exploits the level of the reader is elevated, increasing his or her desire to build a connection with the angelic heavenly realm to which these saints were and are connected.

It is hoped through this humble work you, our dear reader, will come to better understand the inner teachings of the Sufi Way in Islam; namely, the practice of moderation, compassion, to follow the middle course, to hold patience, to uphold tolerance and respect for others and to avoid conflicts through peaceful means of approach. Terrorism, on the other hand, stands condemned by every ethical person as one of today's most terrible evils. Above all, our Grandshaykh's teachings are to love God, appreciate His Divine favors, and strive in His service. The greatest Sufi teaching is that there is no higher station than serving the Lord Almighty and serving God's creation, human beings.

I would like to particularly thank my daughter, Hajjah Nazihe Adil, and those who labored hard with Shaykh Hisham to bring this volume to print.

As my deputy, who is entrusted with the secrets of the Golden Chain and the support of the Naqshbandi Masters, I pray for Shaykh Hisham's success in quickly bringing a second volume to print, which will further elaborate the miracles, discipline, and Divine powers inherent in the Naqshbandi Sufi Way, whose access is guaranteed through sincerity, devotion, and the purification of hearts.

Shaykh Muhammad Nazim Adil al-Haqqani
Lefke, Cyprus
12 Rabi al-Awwal, 1426
21 April, 2005

# THE GOAL OF SAINTS AND MASTERS

*[A talk given to a group of Gurdjieff students.]*

Our Grandshaykh spoke often about the master, Gurdjieff; of the closeness he felt towards him and how, after Gurdjieff died, his student John Bennett used to come frequently to see him. Gurdjieff met Grandshaykh 'Abd Allah ad-Daghestani ق at least once. Some of John Bennett's followers, as well as his son, met our master Shaykh Nazim.

All masters are one in this universe. In one family all members are the same. In our belief, if you meet this master or that, it is the same; for all of them receive their power from the One who is the center of all things, whose name in Arabic is Allah, God, our Lord.

Master Gurdjieff met our master secretly. Our Grandshaykh wished nothing to be known of that meeting and therefore it was kept secret. All that was mentioned in Gurdjieff's books was that he met some saints in Damascus and Baghdad with no mention of their names. Still, he ordered John Bennett to meet with our Grandshaykh frequently and allowed him to mention these meetings in his books. That is why John Bennett spoke about Grandshaykh.

On the occasion of their secret meeting, Grandshaykh gave permission to Gurdjieff to use the power of the Nine Points, with which many in the west are familiar. However, he did not give Gurdjieff permission to use all that spiritual power and he did not pass the full measure of the power he received on to his followers.

Even what Grandshaykh gave Gurdjieff from the power of the Nine Points was like the image in a mirror—a reflection of the original. Its secret he kept in his heart. Why? Because he knew that at the end of time a spiritual personality would appear who would use that power in its untainted fullness throughout the earth. That time will be the Golden Age of perfection. When that age arrives everything will attain spiritual fruition and absolute perfection. Today all masters and saints in this universe await that miraculous age. In this time however, the secret of that power is withheld by those who possess it, for its time has not yet come.

We live now in a time of darkness. Saints today do not display the power they have been granted, power by which, in an instant, they are able to change the heart of every human being from negativity and destructiveness to sincerity and virtue. Why do they not use that power?

That power was bestowed on them as a favor from God, as an honor. Saints have the power to bring everyone into their circles but they do not use it because they have not been given permission to do so.

Look today at the number of people following Gurdjieff, or following my master, or any master today. Do they amount to one thousand; 50,000; 100,000; one million? Consider then how many people there are in this world. If they are not following a master in whose hands have they been left? Have they been forgotten or left aside? Impossible.

That power is granted to saints for specific purposes—not to be used everywhere and on every occasion. That is the reason why saints in this time see only certain people—special ones. Just as you cannot find diamonds everywhere due to their rarity, so too are the followers of saints very rare. They are often compared to stars on moonless nights. Such bright stars however are heralds for a golden age to come when this one comes to its end. On that day, followers of saints will shine forth and all masters will come together and use the miraculous power granted to them by God for its intended purpose. On that day, everywhere in this world peace will reign.[i]

For that reason Gurdjieff did not fully unfold the secret that was in his heart, but used only part of it. Many saints have passed away having used only a portion of the secrets granted to them. Yet there will come a time at the end of this world when that one who is to come will restore everything to its proper state.

You and I have been created by our Lord. He has not left us alone to ourselves. In everything, we are equal. Human beings are equal in everything: both women and men. Neither "man" nor "woman" is found in the term "human being." That term includes everyone without discrimination. God did not say, "This is a man, this is a woman." He said "human beings." God said "I sent prophets, saints and spiritual masters as a mercy for human beings." He did not say, "I send saints and prophets for men," or, "I send saints and prophets for women." That is why there are women who are considered saints and men who are considered saints. In God's Eyes there is no discrimination. Everyone is equal. Each human being has a light in his or her heart—the light of sainthood.

God has created us with love. He did not create us for hellfire. When we who have children see them do something wrong, we try to correct them. We do not burn them. We do not put them in the fire. We do not strike them, for even that is not allowed. We only try to correct them, by telling them "this is right; this is wrong." God did not create human beings for punishment.

Many people nowadays claim this, but it is not true. They are showing a cruel side of human nature which is evil and springs from Satan. God is merciful, God is loving, God is light. He created us with His mercy and love. Why are we not using that love and mercy from which we were created, for which we were created, and out of which God molded us, to reach out to others?

If a woman loves a man or a man loves a woman, you will find one near the door of the other. Both desire nothing but to reach their beloved. Not for one second do they wish to be left without some connection to their beloved. When two persons love each other, they are always together. What then about God, who put such love in our hearts in the first place, Who possesses all love; Who in fact, has Oceans of love? Do you not think that He loves you? He loves everyone! The love which God put in our hearts, that brings human beings together, originates from Him and is completely in His Hands.

What then about Him? Does He not love the servant Whom He created with His own Hands? Why are we not using that love and coming to Him? Why are we not seeking to open those secrets our Lord has planted in our hearts?

Sometimes a person leaves this world childless. However, if that person loves someone unrelated to him, before dying that person will write a will bequeathing everything he owns to the one he loves. This comes from love. God loves us. He created us and He is giving us everything. Why are we not taking what He is giving us and using it? On the contrary, most people are distancing themselves from these bequests.

For that reason God sent prophets and messengers, and after them saints, masters of this universe. There are 124,000 saints on this earth, running here and there to look into people's hearts and bring them back to God. It is for that reason that saints know each other and meet with one another.

## The Power of Saintly Hearing

We learn from our masters by listening. However there are levels of hearing and from one level to another there is a vast distance. Masters give according to the level of the disciple. For at one level, "to hear" means what enters the ears, is transmitted to the mind as sound and interpreted as words.

At the next level, "hearing" means when the master speaks, one sees what he is speaking about, taking place before you. The next level is when you hear, see, and feel the events he is describing. At that level it is complete. In fact even then, perception is still not total. Only when you hear, see, feel, taste and smell, then it is complete—then you are experiencing that event as "your" event and you thus become a "witness" to that event.

Nowadays many people read books avidly. Others are constantly on the computer or Internet experiencing what is there. One of my students always has a computer in front of him. Once I asked him, "Do you have Beethoven in there?" He said, "Yes, the Fifth Symphony," and played it for me.

However from a computer you can only hear; you cannot see. You cannot feel as if you were in an auditorium with Beethoven leading the orchestra. So where is Beethoven? You can only hear the sound of those playing the music. However when a master says, "I heard from my master," it means "by means of my shaykh's power I witnessed such and such event."

Similarly everything in this mortal life is merely a reflection of its eternal realities. Our ultimate realities are in the Presence of our Lord. In this respect, do not think that you are ever away from your Lord. It is just as when you look into a mirror and see your own image, but where is your reality? In the Presence of Our Lord we exist in a real fashion. Here, we do not truly exist. Here, our existence is imitative.

The question that arises then is, "When do we truly exist?" The answer is, "When our images conform to our realities."

The aim of saints and spiritual masters is to take you back to your essential self. That is why they speak and write books seeking to reach out and teach humankind.

The power of a saint is not that you take his book and simply read it. When you read a conventional book, you do not feel, nor do you see—you are only reading, generating imaginary images. From a saint you must receive power directly from his heart, not from the words on the paper. The power saints possess is such that when one of them speaks, you cannot help hearing, seeing, smelling and sensing it.

When you observe people who study spiritual teachings on their own, but who do not actually follow a guide, you find them alienated, ill-at-ease. The power saints possess is communicated to the hearts of their followers and manifested in them as a group. Thus a group of people following a saint will be united.

Saints are like the circumference of a circle. The circle is composed of points. On its circumference there are countless points. Yet the circle's center consists of but a single point, and from that point each saint receives light and power. The radii of the circle extend to every point on the circumference, but the distance from the center to each point on the circumference is identical. Each point on the circumference is one saint, one here and another there. Each saint takes from the center. All on the circumference are brothers and sisters—there is no difference between them. When they reach this level, each knows and recognizes the other. But outside this level, humans do not know each other. That is why 124,000 saints know each other, for all of them swimming in the same orbit. That is the meaning of the verse from God's Holy Words:

### *Each one is swimming in his orbit.*[2]

The illustrious saints swim in the orbit of the 124,000, taking from the Center of everything, God most High. If you hold the hand of any one of them it is as if you are holding the hand of all. When you reach one, it is as if you have reached them all. At that time, the light they all possess will be bestowed on you and illuminate your heart.

---

[2] The Holy Qur'an, chapter (Surah) Ya Sin, 36; verse 40; henceforth simply denoted Surah Ya Sin, 36:40.

All masters are striving to send that light to our hearts. But because we are sunk in the life of this material world, the light that reaches us is very dim. Consider this example. A television with an antenna may receive a distorted, hazy picture due to interference from outside. Similarly, when interference from this material world enters your heart, the light you receive will be distorted. For some people, the picture is clear; for some, the picture is hazy. Whether our image is clear or distorted depends upon the quality of our receiver.

All spiritual masters are trying to reach us with the light and the power that God gave them. The master to whom you are affiliated is reaching out to you with the Divine Power God gave him. The problem is that <u>we</u> are not using that power. If we were, we would find ourselves swimming in the same orbit as our master. There cannot be different orbits, for each one is directed to the Divine Presence. Why then are we different? We are not different: only egos are different. Reality itself is never different.

Spirituality is the same for all, for it is from God. If He makes my spiritual nature different from your spiritual nature or any other's spiritual nature, then that would be discrimination. Then there would be no justice on this earth. That is why spirits are never different from each other. That is also why God has said:

> ***We have made you nations and tribes in order that you will know each other.***[3]

When you know each other you are swimming in that ocean of love. If we hold on hatred and enmity amongst ourselves, how are we going to know each other? We are then going against what the

---

[3] Suratu 'l-Hujurat, 49:13.

prophets and messengers of God, particularly the Prophet Muhammad, peace and blessings of God be upon him,[4] has said:

> *Spirits are assembled troops. When they come to each other, they know they come from the same origin.*[5]

Spiritually, we have the same origin but the negative aspect of our ego is trying to destroy us. Everyone's selfish ego makes him or her believe, "I am the only one who should be known; who should be famous; the only one who possesses the truth; the only one who should have wealth and own cars; the only one who should be listened to." The ego aggrandizes everything to itself. If only we would heed our spirit this would never occur. Our spirit informs us that one can listen to a child and receive wisdom. The essence of justice is, "Do not reject anyone!" If you listen to the inspirations of the spirit, you can take wisdom from everything. If you listen to the voice of your ego, you will achieve nothing except hatred, pride, and enmity.

## Seclusion

Once a very famous orientalist came to our Grandmaster Shaykh 'Abd Allah ad-Daghestani ق in Damascus and said:

> O my master, I'm coming to you after studying the Psalms, the Torah, the Bible, and the Holy Qur'an. I've studied all kinds of philosophy and all the religions and every belief that has appeared. But still, I feel nothing in my heart—no satisfaction. On the contrary, it is as if I were standing on the edge of a cliff about to fall. I have become so shaky that

---

[4] Peace and Blessings of God be upon him: This salutation, uttered after each mention of a prophet of God, is henceforth symbolized by ﷺ.
[5] Related in Bukhari from A'isha ؓ, Ahmad, Muslim and Abu Dawud related it from Abu Hurayrah ؓ. At-Tabarani in his *Kabir* from Ibn Mas'ud. Al-Hafiz as-Suyuti declared it sound.

I am going from one spiritual teaching center to another, seeking what is real, trying to find truth. Where can I reach that reality and gain satisfaction in my heart? Where can I find my Lord?

Finally, I have come to you. After you, I am not going anywhere else. I have been everywhere. I have asked famous philosophers, orientalists, people whom I considered saints. I have read everything I could. Yet when I asked any scholar a question, I felt that they gave me an answer I already knew. They were not giving me anything new, anything fresh. Therefore I have lapsed into confusion. I heard your name and I have come to you. Will you give me an answer to my question? Whatever you say, I will follow and believe. But if you do not give me an answer, I shall remain as I am: confused and uncertain for the rest of my life."

Grandshaykh 'Abd Allah responded:

My son, if you take the seed of an apple or any fruit and leave it where it is dry for hundreds of years, it will remain dry. But if you take that seed and put it in a field and plant it, then come back after one month, you will find that a green sprout has come out. If you dig and try to find that seed, you will not find it anymore. It has vanished. But something new is there. If you continue to water that plant it will become a tree and that tree will give fruit. But where is the original seed? It has disappeared. That seed has become a large tree now, giving people fruit to eat.

Similarly, if you take an egg and put it under a chicken for twenty-one days, after exactly twenty-one days, that egg disappears and a new chick emerges. Something new comes into being. If you look under the chicken you will no longer find the egg there. The egg has vanished. It was under that chicken for twenty-one days and then it turned into a new generation. Something similar happens with human beings within their mother's womb for about nine months and ten days, separated from everything outside, alone. Yet after those nine months and ten days of loneliness, out will come a new generation; a new creation.

My son, in each of these three examples I have given you there was something that went into seclusion. The seed cut itself off from the material world above the ground and went into seclusion for thirty, forty or fifty days; then a new plant emerged. The egg went into seclusion under its mother with no connection to the material life outside its shell and after twenty-one days comes out a new generation. The sperm and egg went into seclusion in the mother's womb for nine months and ten days, without connection to the external world of this materialistic life. But after this seclusion a new generation emerged.

My son, if you do not enter into seclusion and say to yourself just as that seed says to itself, "I want to cut myself off from the materialistic life of this world and vanish from it for the love of God and for the benefit of other human beings"—for the seed begets fruit—if you do not experience a retreat like this, if you do not cut yourself off from the material life, forsake your ego in complete sacrifice and vanish into nothingness, to exist only in God, never will you find your ultimate reality, your true self. Never will you be like that tree that gives fruit for people to eat. If you will not to be like that egg and sever yourself from materialism, retreating into the shell of seclusion and existing only in the presence of your Lord, meditating, concentrating on Him, worshipping Him, keeping His presence always in your heart, never will you find that happiness and satisfaction which you seek.

Why must you imitate that sperm that enters into seclusion for nine months with the egg? It is because the mother's womb consists of three layers—something mentioned fourteen hundred years ago in the Holy Qur'an at a time when no microscopes existed. The Prophet ﷺ revealed that the womb of a mother is made of "darknesses," that is, layers.[6] Hence, if you enter not into this loneliness, severing your bond to everything external, cutting yourself off from the material things of this world to be alone with your Lord, and thus make connection to your ultimate reality by fitting the image with which you are dressed here to its original there in the Divine Presence, never will you know satisfaction, no matter how many books you read. For when you read, you only "hear" the books. The knowledge they contain is only "heard of" knowledge and thus not real. Yet in seclusion, you not only hear but you feel, you will not only see, but you smell. It is then that the eyes of the heart open. My son, if you do not enter into seclusion, your heart will never feel the contentment you have been seeking so long.

Immediately, the scholar said, "You have given the right answer. My heart is open. Show me the way." Then Grandshaykh gave him permission to enter into seclusion in a certain place, cutting himself off from everything.[ii] The scholar entered that place an ordinary man but after one year, he came out a saint.

## Gurdjieff's Pursuit of Spiritual Masters

Master Gurdjieff was seeking reality. That is why he was looking for saints, the "remarkable men" of whom he spoke. He

---

[6] He makes you, in the wombs of your mothers, in stages, one after another, in three veils of darkness. such is God, your Lord and Cherisher: to Him belongs (all) dominion. (Suratu 'z-Zumar, 39:6)

sought them in order to find reality, and he found it. Anyone who seeks out saints will be a saint[iii], for like is drawn to like: if a person is not of that kind, he or she will not seek them. Master Gurdjieff kept seeking out saints because from his childhood a certain light illumined his heart, urging him to increase its brightness until he attained his reality. God be praised, and may He bless him and us, he found that reality through the many saints he met in the Middle East, in the Far East, and wherever he traveled. When he met with Grandshaykh secretly, he was dressed with the raiment of sainthood; he was granted permission and was ordered to use a portion of the miraculous power bestowed on his heart sufficiently to influence people. The fullness of the power he was given will appear only at the end of this age.

All saints today—whether living or passed on—are waiting for expected tremendous changes on earth. Now, those saints who are yet alive await those events which signal the golden age before us. We pray our Lord grant us life to witness that time. At that time, all will see saints together and it will be the happiest time ever seen on earth. At that time hatred and enmity will disappear. Saints will come together and people will follow them. This will last for a period of forty years. After that era of perfection, another period of decline will set in and the end of this world will be upon us.

We are ordered to be humble. We are ordered to respect everyone without discrimination. We keep everyone high in our regard and thus God keeps us high in His regard.

Once, Bayazid al-Bistami ق, one of the greatest saints of old, was drawing nigh to the door of his Lord, to the Divine Presence with the power that he had developed in his heart through years of self-discipline and meditation. When he finally attained the threshold of the door to the Divine Presence, he called out, "O my Lord, please open the door and let me see You!" The answer came through his heart, "O Bayazid, you cannot see Me. It is an easy thing to come to the door, but it is not easy for the door of My Divine Presence to be opened for you. It has a price." Bayazid replied, "O my Lord, what is the price? I am even willing to sacrifice my life for it. Only let me come to You." He heard the reply, "O Bayazid, My price is that you have to go back and become a refuse heap, a place where My servants throw their garbage."

This means, "Carry the burdens of My servants." If you carry people's burdens, making no discrimination between them, you can never say, "This one is white; that one is black; this one is yellow; that one is red; or this or that." No! All are human beings. Once you accept this fact and go and become a carrier of people's burdens, Allah says, "I will open My Divine Presence to you."

Bayazid al-Bistami ق went back and for seven years worked to carry people's burdens by taking their sins on his shoulders. He was coming to his Lord and praying:

> O my Lord, I come to Thee. Whatever You will to do with me, do! As for others, leave them in rest and peace. If You will punishment for them—while I know there is no punishment—but if You will it, let me alone receive Thy punishment and let everyone else go free. I shall take their punishment on myself. O Lord! Make my body as wide as hell and as deep, that I might enter that space and fill it and so no one else may enter.

This is for love of God. If you love your Lord, you love His servants. What benefit is there in loving my Lord or in loving my master if I don't love his devotees? That is not true love. True love is to love both your master and his followers. This is the proof that love is true. If you love your Lord with a true love, you must love everyone without discrimination, for He created all of them. But where do you find such love on earth? This frame of mind only exists with saintly people and their followers.[iv] Outside this saintly circle, everyone is fighting one another in enmity and hatred. For that reason, wherever you go, you must be messengers of peace, love and respect.

Thank you for your attention and thank you for your visit. Your coming here is an extreme honor for us. It has always been my dream to meet the followers of Gurdjieff because I did not have an opportunity to see him, but only heard about him from my Grandshaykh and from my shaykh. Once I saw his student, John Bennett. I was very young then and I met him with Grandshaykh while in Damascus. A lady was with him, his secretary at the time. But that was a very long time ago. Thank you again for coming.

**Question:** I heard this quote perhaps ten years ago: *Adhlaluna arwahuna, arwahuna adhlaluna*.

**Shaykh Hisham:** It is true. It means that our shadows, *adhlaluna*, are our spirits, *arwahuna*. But when? When you have that connection. Look at the mirror now and you see your reflection. It is an image of yourself. Or if the sun is out, you see your shadow. If we can see the shadow, we know that there is an origin, a body, a shape, or else that shadow would never appear. Now the shadow points to the spirit—*adhlaluna arwahuna*—our shadows signify our spirits. Our spirits are always in the Divine Presence. Our shadows are here, on this earth. When we can make that connection, we find our path. That is why saints come: to show you your path. When you find your path, you can see your spirit there, through your "shadow." Then you have that connection. And when you have that connection, at that time "our shadows are our spirits and our spirits are our shadows" becomes true. Only at that time is there no separation and they are together. And at that time you are not blind, your eyes are open. But till then, we are blind.

Al-Junayd ق was one of the greatest saints. In twenty-four hours, he was in the presence of his Lord at every moment. He was never separated. He was always receiving, taking from Him all the day long. All saints are that way. That is why I gave you the example of the circle: it has a circumference and a center. No point of the circumference is off center at any time. At every moment, they are equidistant, taking from the center. This is a geometric fact, a truth of mathematics.

We hope to be follow Junayd ق—to imitate him. We cannot be like him, he is very high. But we ask our Lord that through Junayd ق we can reach even that height. We must use all means necessary to come to our Lord.

**Question:** When you talk about withdrawing into seclusion every day, should I understand people coming together for their own practice or worship, or one person alone? Are these two different types of seclusion?

**Shaykh Hisham:** They are two different types. But that doesn't mean that collective retreat is not seclusion. When people come together for their practice, it is considered a seclusion. When they sit together, practicing what their master ordered them, this is seclusion. But the higher level is to be alone, to separate oneself from everything. When you sit with people around you, sometimes you will be disturbed. Perhaps you are sitting in this hall, and a person will be coming inside to join you. There will be a disturbance in the heart. But when you are sitting alone, with the doors closed, no one will disturb you. Nothing is between you and your Lord. For some portion of time—not forever. That seclusion is for a certain time, to train you. When you sever yourself from life, it is to train you. After that time, when you sit with your group, with your brothers and sisters, all of you will be more powerful in keeping back any disturbances.

Now, as we sit together, this is considered a seclusion because we are not mentioning anything about the outside, materialistic life. We are only speaking about those things which connect us to our realities. As he has something to repeat [pointing to the person who asked the first question], *adhlaluna arwahuna, arwahuna adhlaluna,* in seclusion you will be given something to repeat many times, because you have to ride a vehicle, use a means, in order to reach your destination. You will be given something to ride on in order to find your reality—your spirit.

This [pointing to himself] is a cage; your body is a cage. When you break that cage, your spirit is free. Then you can be everywhere. Until that time, you have to work to break it. How do you break it? You cannot break it except through seclusion, by sitting together or sitting alone, practicing to break that cage. When you break that cage—finished. You can be with people outside, you can be with people inside, you are free. Your spirit is free.

# REMEMBER YOUR LORD

***Obey God, obey the Prophet, and obey those in authority among you.[7]***

We are in a time in which wherever one looks, there is confusion and corruption. We are in a time in which life is very difficult. Everyone is running after the materialistic life. No one thinks of the eternal life. Everyone is thinking about this life only—how to make more money, generate greater income, and enjoy a higher standard of living.

Now no one is saying you should not generate more income in order to live at a high standard. God wants you to live a pleasant life. God created you in this world and told you, "Live a good life." But He also said, "Do not forget Me."

If you are going to forget your Lord, what is the use of this life? God has created us to know Him. He did not create us to run after money.[8] He created us to know Him, and to take our share and portion of this life. So if you need to generate income, make money. You must live life, so live it. But don't forget your Lord. If you have one hour for your own life, you must have another hour for your Lord. And nowadays no one is asking for one hour for his or her Lord. A minute is enough! In these times, no one is willing to give even a single minute of one's his time for his Lord. Everyone in this life is running after money twenty-four hours a

---

[7] Suratu 'n-Nisa, 4:59.

[8] Jesus ﷺ said: The head of every iniquity is the love of the world. (Al-Hafiz as-Suyuti related it in his commentary on the Holy Qur'an)

day and even then they are not stopping. Still, God said, in the Holy Qur'an:

> ***I have created spiritual beings and human beings only to worship Me.***[9]

All the Messengers came to tell you, "Worship your Lord." They did not say, "Worship money."

## Underground Idol

There was once a saint famous throughout the Muslim world whose books are studied until this day in all universities where philosophy or Sufi teachings are taught. His name is Muhyiddin ibn 'Arabi.

One day he said, "What you worship is under my feet."[10] Scholars at the time understood that Muhyiddin Ibn 'Arabi ق was saying, "Your Lord is under my feet." In actuality he was saying, "The object you worship is under my feet," not "your Lord." So they said, "That person must be hanged for heresy," and they killed him. Even though they sought to kill him, he did not say "No." He accepted God's will and said, "If God wants me to pass away and sacrifice my life for the benefit of human beings, I am willing." Ibn 'Arabi's secret was not revealed except after his death. They dug under the spot where he uttered this famous phrase and there they found a huge treasure of gold. That treasure was under his feet.

From the beginning of time people have been chasing money. No one is thinking that God has created us in this life to worship Him. We are not saying don't live a decent life. Live a comfortable life. God gave you this beautiful world, nature. Enjoy it. But also worship Him, remember Him in your heart.

---

[9] Suratu 'dh-Dhariyat, 51:56.
[10] Arabic: ma'budakum tahta qadamee.

## Holding Fire

Is anyone remembering his Lord? How many people are here? We are thirty or forty people. Yet how many thousands and millions are outside? Who is remembering God? Very few people are keeping that remembrance. That is why in the Last Days, the Prophet ﷺ said there will come a time when:

> Anyone who grasps his religion firmly and faithfully will be like one grasping a burning coal.[11]

Who is holding fast to his religion today? Only a few people. Why? Because most are busy chasing the material things of this world. No one is thinking that Moses ﷺ came and preached One Lord; Jesus ﷺ came and preached One Lord, and Prophet Muhammad ﷺ came and preached One Lord. Everyone today however, is preaching his ego, he considers his ego his lord. No one is considering as his God the One who is in heaven. Each one is saying, "No, I am God! There is no god except me!—*La ilaha illa ana*," instead of saying, "*La ilaha ill-Allah*—There is no god except God." That is why no one is listening to the Lord of Creation; everyone is listening to his or her ego.

If you invite anyone to attend a place of worship, he will say, "I have no need to go." Why is there no need? If you don't want to go to a place of worship, at least make a room in your house a place of worship. Sit by yourself, alone with your Lord. Sit and ask forgiveness. God is merciful. He is not about making people afraid of Him. Indeed, it is He who said in the Qur'an:

> ***I am the Merciful One, I am the Forgiver!*[12]**

"I am The Concealer, as-Sattar! I hide the sins of My servants. But let them come and ask Me for forgiveness."

---

[11] Tirmidhi, Ahmad, al-Hakim.
[12] Suratu 'l-Hijr, 15:49.

## Forgive and be Forgiven

God asks us to forgive each other, by saying in the Qur'an:

***Whoever forgives and makes peace takes his reward from God.*** [13]

If God lays down this order for us, what about Himself? If someone harmed us or hurt us, He asks us to forgive that person and make peace.[v] Is it not even more the case that He will treat us in a forgiving manner; is He not going to forgive us when we come to Him? He is waiting for one step from you in order to come towards you ninety-nine steps.

Come towards God one step, and He will move ninety-nine steps towards you. Only turn to Him with repentance and ask forgiveness. Say, "O our Lord, the Merciful One, we are coming to Your Mercy. Forgive us." He is the Just One, the One who is always true. His Justice is apparent everywhere. He created us. Do you think He created us and abandoned us to our egoes? God is never going to leave one of His human beings. He created us with His Hands in order to forgive us in the end.[vi] So turn to Him at least one time and say, "O my Lord, forgive me."

The Prophet ﷺ said in a well-known tradition (hadith)[14] that if you commit the same sin seventy times daily, and every time, you turn to your Lord and ask for forgiveness, God will forgive you. God said to the Prophet ﷺ in the Qur'an:

***Say: "O My servants who have transgressed against their souls do not despair of the mercy of God, God is the One who forgives and erases all***

---

[13] Suratu 'sh-Shura, 42:40.

[14] Hadith: (pl. ahadith), a saying or relation or tradition reported from the mouth of the Prophet ﷺ or from his behavior.

> sins; He is the Oft-Forgiving, the Owner of Mercy."[15]

Those who have *"transgressed against their own souls"* are those who are busy in pursuing their desires and pleasures without end. Where then are we? We are running away. Why are you running away? God is giving us provision. He is providing for each one, without looking at whether he is a doer of badness or of goodness; a positive influence or a negative destructive one. Observe: you will see tyrants in good health, eating, drinking, and doing whatever they like, just as you see good people also being provided for. God is not looking at our behavior; God is being merciful with us.

> *I have not created jinn and human beings except to worship Me. I do not want sustenance from them, and I do not want them to feed Me. God is the Provider; of Unbreakable Might.*[16]

God is the One providing everything to human beings, without looking at their races, or colors—without discrimination. In God's Eyes, everyone is equal. With God, inequality does not exist. In the eyes of the Lord, there is no white, no black, no brown, no yellow, no red. All are the same, human beings—can anyone say they are not? All come from one father and one mother. Why then are they creating enmity and hatred among themselves?[vii]

So come to your Lord, come to God—if you believe in Him. If not, this is something else. But if you believe there is one God in Heaven, whether you are Jewish, Christian, Muslim—whatever you are—come to your Lord. God does not change. He is the Lord

---

[15] Suratu 'z-Zumar, 39:53.
[16] Suratu 'dh-Dhariyat, 51:56-58.

of the Jews, the Lord of the Christians and Lord of the Muslims., Lord of people of all faiths. Turn to Him. Don't run away. If you turn away from His Mercy, no one will grant you mercy except Him Whose characteristic is to be ever-merciful. Do not think that there is someone else who is going to be merciful with you or forgive you your sins except Him.

## The Unmanned Ship

Once some men of learning came to Sayyidina 'Ali ﷺ, the fourth Caliph of the Prophet ﷺ who was his cousin as well as his son-in-law. They were neither Muslim nor Christian scholars, but philosophers. They were asking Sayyidina 'Ali ﷺ questions and he was answering them. Finally, they spoke out and said, "There is no God." He said, "I cannot give you an answer here, let us go to the seashore."

They went to the Red Sea in Jeddah. Sayyidina 'Ali ﷺ was sitting on the sea-shore, and those philosophers were with him. He looked across to the horizon and saw a ship making its way to the shore.

He said, "O, I am astonished! There is no captain on that ship and no crew, and that ship is coming by itself to shore. What miraculous power!"

"Are you crazy? Are you saying that ship has no captain and crew to make it come to land?"

"Yes—because I am not seeing either a captain and crew for that ship, so it is apparent to me that the ship is coming ashore by itself."

"We thought you were a wise man. It turns out that you are not wise at all."

"Why are you jumping to this conclusion? Wait until the ship arrives. If there is indeed a captain and a crew, then you may say that I am not wise."

Since this was a reasonable condition, they agreed to wait. After several hours the ship reached port. Out of the ship emerged a captain and crew.

The philosophers looked at Sayyidina 'Ali ؊ and said, "Didn't we say that you are not a wise? You said that ship was coming here by itself and now you see this crew and this captain?"

He said, "Yes, I saw."

Then, they said, "But you said before 'that ship has no captain or crew.'"

He said, "For that ship, you accept that there has to be a captain and an entire crew of men. But to govern this universe, you are not accepting even one Lord!"

If a comet changes its orbit by even a single second, everyone on this earth becomes afraid it will hit us. But who is keeping the stars in their orbits? Who is maintaining these distances between moons and suns, between galaxies? Is it by chance, by accident?[17] Some say everything has been created by chance! *Subhanallah*—Glory be to God! How crazy they are.

They say, "Men came from monkeys." One hundred years from now they will say men came from donkeys. This is what they are going to say; and a little bit later, they will say, "we are coming from mosquitoes!"

Everyone must remember his Lord in his heart. God has created us in order to know Him. This is why He said in a Holy Tradition (*hadith qudsi*):[18]

---

[17] In other words, the proof of God's existence is the appearance of creation and it is also a proof of His power (*qudrah*) to manifest creation. As for the orbits of moons, planets and stars, they are the proof of His pre-existence (*qidam*) in the calculations of their motion.

[18] *hadith qudsi*: a Divine Saying reported by the Prophet.

> *I was a hidden treasure and I wanted to be known, so I created Creation.*[19]

If the Lord did not create us, how would we know Him? This is the wisdom of our creation: to know our Lord! That is why He brought about this creation.

## The Philosophers and the Child Imam

In olden times, they used to hold debates between scholars and philosophers. If one group of scholars defeated another in debate, the losing group was obliged to follow the beliefs of the winners.

One time, some philosophers came to the sultan, Harun ar-Rashid, and said, "We have come to debate your scholars," with the understanding that if they won the debate his scholars would be obliged to follow their beliefs and vice versa. The scholars were secular—not believers in God; neither Jewish, nor Christian, nor Muslim, nor of any other faith.

Sultan Harun ar-Rashid then had a dream in which he saw Prophet Muhammad ﷺ coming to him accompanied by Jesus Christ ﷺ, telling him that the only one capable to debate these scholars is Imam Shafi'i[20] and commanding him to call that famous Imam to the debate. At the time, however, Imam Shafi'i was only thirteen years old. He was a young child, and yet was expected to debate people forty, fifty and sixty years of age.

After seeing that dream, Harun ar-Rashid immediately called Imam Shafi'i and told him to debate those people. At the assigned place and time, these scholars were sitting in the presence of many

---

[19] Razi, Suyuti, Jarrahi, Ibn 'Iraq.
[20] Imam Shafi'i was founder of one of the four Sunni schools of Islamic jurisprudence. The other three imams are: Malik, Abu Hanifa and Ahmad bin Hanbal.

people and Imam Shafi'i, a young child, entered and sat opposite them. The scholars of the secular group thought that this was Imam Shafi'i's son, whom he had sent ahead with some news for them. So they said to him, "Son, where is your father, the scholar? Why are you sitting there?"

Imam Shafi'i answered, "Iraq is a big ocean of scholars. Why should they lose their time debating you? They sent me instead; because a child is enough for you, and we don't need anyone else to debate you." This is an example of the hadith, "War is deception."[21]

You have to dupe your opponent; by saying this the scholars immediately grew fearful. When a child of thirteen says such a thing, he undermines his opponents' power, for if they debate this child and defeat him, they still have to contend with his father. What will happen then? So their power was immediately reduced by half.

And so they began to ask him questions, and he responded with the answers right on the spot, one after another. Finally, they said, "All right, we accept all you have said; but let us see Allah. Let us see God. If you show us God, we will accept. If you don't show us God, we will not!"

How was he to show them God? Sayyidina Imam Shafi'i then said to the king—who was happy with all his answers—"O my king, I am hearing someone selling milk outside. Order someone to go and bring me that milk." The king was so happy that he did not even wait to give the order but went outside himself. When he left the place where the people were sitting in debate, he looked round and saw no one selling milk. What had Imam Shafi'i heard if there was no one there? Harun ar-Rashid waited and waited. After ten minutes, he saw someone coming, carrying milk.

---

[21] Bukhari and Muslim.

Imam Shafi'i had seen someone coming from afar with the eyes of his heart—not with the eyes of his head. Eyes of flesh see nothing except what's located in the same room. They cannot see behind a wall.

But the spiritual eyes of the heart can see even behind walls. That is why all prophets and all saints are able to speak about the future.[viii] God gave everyone that power, but we are not using it. Use it, and God will give you 'power upon power' and more besides.[ix] But you must remember Him in your heart in order that He will remember you.[x] If you are going to remember only money and pleasure, God will never remember you.

Harun ar-Rashid took the milk from that person and brought it to young Imam Shafi'i. The Imam called the biggest of the scholars and said to him, "O my father—out of respect—I am asking you: is there cheese in that milk?" The secular scholar said "Yes!" The Imam asked, "Is there butter in that milk?" He said "Yes!" The Imam asked, "Is there water?" He said "Yes!" The Imam said, "Show me!" The scholar answered, "How can I show it to you? It needs a special process in order to separate the milk, the butter, the cheese and the water." The Imam then said, "If you need a process for this milk, how then are you going to see the Lord of Heavens without a process? You have to follow a way, a path, a religion in order to come and see your Lord. But someone like me, who has the eyes of his heart open, can say, 'In the Name of God, the Compassionate, the Merciful, *Bismillahi 'r-rahmani 'r-rahim,*' and they will separate."

At this, the cheese separated from the milk, the butter separated out, and the water was left. He continued, "Someone who has these eyes can see his Lord. But someone like you can never see his Lord, except by going through a process."

One scholar immediately asked, "What kind of process? Show it to me and I will accept." He was convinced. The young Imam said, "The process is to believe in God and to believe in all His prophets—Noah, Abraham, Moses, Jesus Christ and Muhammad, peace be on them all. If you believe in these five messengers and in all other prophets, at that time, you are going to see your Lord.[xi] At that time, your heart is going to be enlightened and filled with light, not full of hatred and enmity.[xii] You have to believe in His prophets and messengers. If you don't believe, then it is very difficult for you to know your Lord."

## God's Servants are Equal

The Lord has made everyone equal, by saying in Qur'an:

> **The best among you are the most God-wary or righteous,**[22]

and the Prophet ﷺ said in his last sermon:

> *There is no superiority of Arab over non-Arab except in righteousness.*[23]

This means people of color, or white people, whoever is God-wary or righteous, that one is going to be foremost. Whoever is corrupt will be left behind. If you want to be in the forefront, you have to be good people.

What is the meaning of "good people?" Good people must not have hatred, enmity or inequity towards anyone of God's servants in their hearts. Everyone must be equal in their eyes: this is up to God, it is not your judgment. You cannot judge them.

> *If someone calls a believer in God "unbeliever," he, the speaker, is the unbeliever.*[24]

---

[22] Suratu 'l-Hujurat, 49:13.
[23] Ahmad, Al-Haythami, Ibn Jawzi, As-Suyuti.
[24] At-Tabarani.

This is a saying of the Prophet ﷺ, and this is what we believe. As soon as one believes in God, the matter is finished. The judgment is between a person and his Lord. You have no right against him. Once he says, "There is no god except our Lord in heavens," the case is closed! It is not our duty to oppose him, to fight him, to kill him, or to say bad things about him[xiii]. That is why it is a very grave sin to call anyone *mushrik* or *kafir*—idolater or unbeliever. Judgment belongs only to God, not to us!

We have to keep this in our heart and to know this fact. We must not do as other people who are calling and classifying everyone 'unbelievers.' It is not our duty. You cannot sit on God's Throne. God is God and servant is servant! There is One Lord, and all else are servants. We are all the same. He created them; why are you interfering with Him?

God sent messengers. You have no right to hate people because of their religion. You have no right to fight them because of their religion. You have no right to utter any bad word against them because of their religion. This must be our belief.

God willing, we are beseeching our Lord to open our hearts and to cause us to hear and obey His words, revealed in the Holy Qur'an, the Torah and the New Testament:

> ***Be one hand holding the rope of God, tightly, altogether, and do not separate...***[25]

against corruption and against unbelief.

---

[25] Surat Ali-'Imran, 3:103.

# The Cave of Secrets

The first of Muharram was the date Prophet Muhammad ﷺ was ordered by his Lord to migrate from Makkah to Madinah. Why did the Prophet ﷺ have to migrate? He is a prophet and God is protecting him, and God said that He is protecting Islam until the Last Day. So why did the Prophet ﷺ run away? Prophets never run away. What was the wisdom behind the Prophet ﷺ going from Makkah to Madinah? There must be something hidden there—something hidden in the heart of the Prophet ﷺ.

Did he leave because they came to kill him; because they made a plan to assassinate him? By no means. He only had to throw sand into their eyes, and read the verse:

> **We have placed a barrier in front of them and a barrier behind them, and we have made their eyes unable to see,**[xiv]

and by God's Power they were unable to see him as he left his house. He could as easily have thrown anything on them and finished them off completely, as God protected His Ka'bah in the time of Abraha when Abraha tried to destroy it. The grandfather of the Prophet ﷺ, Sayyidina 'Abd al-Muttalib said, "There is an Owner for that House that is able to protect it." At that time, God protected His Holy House by sending a flock of birds carrying small stones in their beaks and claws. They showered Abraha's army with these pebbles, devastating it.[xv]

Why then did the Prophet ﷺ go from Makkah to Madinah? He was able to ask his Lord to send something on these people and be finished with the ignorant folk who sought to kill him. There are many hidden secrets there.

As we know, according to Divine Law (*Shari'ah*),[26] the Prophet ﷺ went from Makkah to Madinah to build the first government of Islam, the first foundation of Islam, the first light for human beings to be spread from East to West. This is the external explanation—that he went from an unsafe place to a safe place in order to establish the first foundation for Allah's light. From that center, the Prophet ﷺ was to enlighten the hearts of his Companions—*Sahabah*—and the hearts of his Community until the Judgment Day with the message, "O people, run from the torture of your ego and from its negative manners to the positive manners of your spirit, and establish the house of your Lord in your heart on a firm foundation." For the Prophet ﷺ also said:

*The heart of a believer is the house of God.*[27]

Establish that house in your heart. God, Whom neither heaven nor earth can contain, has allowed Himself to be contained within the house of the human heart. What is the foundation of that house? Good manners. When you are a positive person, then God will send that light into your heart. When you are not a positive person but you are trying to be a positive person, God will support you. However, when you never try to be a positive person, Satan will support you. If you like Satan's support, take your support from him. But you will be the loser. If you want your Lord to support you, you are a winner. That is why God said in Qur'an:

**O believers, fear God and be with true people.**[28]

---

[26] *Shari'ah*: the system of Islamic law.
[27] Al-Ghazali, Suhrawardi.
[28] Suratu 't-Tawbah, 9:119.

"Fear God" means seek to do the right thing, to be upright in conduct—because no one must be afraid of his Lord. Allah is the Source of all love and possesses the Oceans of mercy and love.

As one of our brothers here said, let us speak tonight about *sidq*, truthfulness. Who possesses truthfulness? It is very difficult, especially in this time. Very few people have this virtue.[xvi] That is why the above verse from Qur'an said, *"Be with true people."* It did not say, *"Be"* a true person, because it is very difficult to be a true person. But to be *with* true people is easy. This life is a long way to travel by yourself and find the way. So it is easier for us to find a true person and to follow him or her.

### Secret of the Prophet's Stay in the Cave

That is why the Prophet ﷺ migrated from Makkah to Madinah: in order to establish a foundation of true people—his Companions—and that is why they have been called the Companions or *Sahabah* ؓ. They received that title from God. No one can be a Companion of the Prophet ﷺ except those that were with him ﷺ. This is a rank no one can reach. After the Prophet ﷺ, no one has reached the level of being a Companion.

When the Prophet ﷺ migrated from Makkah to Madinah, he was ordered to pass by a cave. According to the Prophetic history (*seerah*) that cave was called Gharu Thawr and lies one day's journey from Makkah. The Prophet ﷺ stayed there for three days. Why did the Prophet ﷺ stay in that cave? He was able to continue. There is a secret that made him stop there.

The Prophet ﷺ was ordered to migrate from Makkah to Madinah for the purpose of entering the cave Gharu Thawr, and that is where God taught him how to make *dhikr*.²⁹ It was the first time that the Prophet, God's blessings and peace upon him, made *dhikr* with a loud voice.^xvii That is a very great Sufi secret indeed.

To migrate from Makkah to Madinah was something very easy for the Prophet ﷺ. He had only to say, "In the name of God, the Compassionate, the Merciful—*Bismillahi 'r-Rahmani 'r-Rahim*," and he was in Madinah; just as easily as he took sand from the ground and threw it in the faces of the ignorant people and thus they he was veiled from their vision as he was left his house. Or he could have ridden a horse or camel and have reached Madinah in ten or fifteen days. Why did he go to that cave, the "Cave of Silence," as some have called it? And, indeed, it is the "Cave of Silent Secrets." Since no one knew about this—why was Prophet ﷺ ordered by God to go to that cave, which is one day away from Makkah, when he had a distance of fifteen days travel to go?

When the Prophet ﷺ went into that cave, a spider spun a web in the cave entrance, and a pair of pigeons came and made a nest there, in order that no one would know what was inside. But this is the common knowledge. As for the secret, look to love. When love for someone is pure, God will never forget that person.

## The Love of Sayyidina Ali

Before leaving Makkah for Madinah, the Prophet ﷺ placed someone in his bed, in order that the ignorant people who came to his door intent on killing him, would not realize he had left. He placed Sayyidina 'Ali ؓ in his bed. On the spiritual level, this means that he made Sayyidina 'Ali ؓ his representative. He did not place any other of his Companions there, but someone of his own flesh and blood. And he took as company on the migration,

---

²⁹*Dhikr*: Remembrance of God; performed by any invocation of the Names of God or declaration of sacred phrases, inwardly or outwardly, spontaneously or repetitively, individually or collectively.

that other image of himself, Sayyidina Abu Bakr ﷺ. He accompanied him to the cave. He ﷺ said:

> *I am the city of knowledge, and 'Ali is the door.*[30]

The door is something physical, external. When you want to enter the house here, how do you enter? Through the door. In order to enter to the Prophet ﷺ and to come to the knowledge that the Prophet ﷺ is giving, you have to enter through the door. That door was Sayyidina 'Ali ﷺ.

The Prophet ﷺ also said:

> *Whatever God has poured into my heart, I poured into the heart of Abu Bakr as-Siddiq ﷺ.*[31]

The Prophet ﷺ also referred to the secret of Abu Bakr ﷺ when he said:

> *Abu Bakr does not surpass you for fasting or praying more but because of a secret that took root in his heart.*[32]

So inside the house, we find Sayyidina Abu Bakr ﷺ and on the house's outside we find Sayyidina 'Ali ﷺ. In the Sufi understanding, the house symbolizes the heart. That is why, of the two Sufi knowledges, one came from Sayyidina Abu Bakr and one from Sayyidina 'Ali ﷺ. From the time of the four *madhahib*,[33] Muslims have affirmed that the knowledge of the heart came from these two sources. Justice and laws, on the other hand, came from Sayyidina 'Umar ﷺ.

---

[30] Tirmidhi. Hakim, Ibn 'Asakir, al-'Iraqi, al-Haythami, as-Suyuti.
[31] Maybudi, Razi, as-Suyuti.
[32] Ahmad al-Ghazali, Hakim.
[33] *Madhahib*: the major schools of legal thought in Islam: Maliki, Shafi'i. Hanafi, Hanbali.

The Prophet's ﷺ saying about Abu Bakr is the secret of the cave. To represent his body, the Prophet ﷺ put Sayyidina 'Ali ؓ in his bed prior to his departure from Makkah to Madinah. This means that Sayyidina 'Ali ؓ was designated for the entrance and into the cave the Prophet ﷺ took with him Sayyidina Abu Bakr ؓ. The cave represents what is interior. In the Qur'an, God is ordering us:

*Enter, resort to the cave! Your Lord will shower His mercies on you and dispose of your affair towards comfort and ease.* [34]

And who is the cave for this Community except the Prophet ﷺ? It is an order for everyone on this earth to run to the cave. Everyone has a cave within his heart which directs him to the great cave, the general cave, which is the heart of the Prophet ﷺ. And that immense cave takes you to the mercy of your Lord.

## The Station of the Veracious One

Who did Sayyidina Muhammad ﷺ choose to go with him to the cave? It was Sayyidina Abu Bakr ؓ, who had been given the title *as-Siddiq*—the Veracious. When the Prophet ﷺ entered the cave, he was very tired. He reclined and placed his head on Abu Bakr as-Siddiq's leg. Who, I ask, can put the head of a prophet upon his leg? Sayyidina Abu Bakr as-Siddiq ؓ bore on his leg the head of the most Beloved One of Allah. This is a high honor for Sayyidina Abu Bakr as-Siddiq ؓ. For us the Prophet ﷺ was sleeping, but for himself, it was an ascension, a *mi'raj*, for the Prophet ﷺ knows no sleep:

*My eyes sleep, but my heart never sleeps.* [35]

---

[34] Suratu 'l-Kahf, 18:16.
[35] Bukhari and Muslim.

His heart never sleeps! His heart is always connected with his Lord. He is always in ascension.

I once heard this from my shaykh who, in turn, heard it from his Grandshaykh:

> People say that the Prophet ﷺ went to his Lord in the Night Journey. According to Naqshbandi teachings and secrets which they took from the heart of Sayyidina Abu Bakr as-Siddiq ؓ, there were twelve thousand night-journeys for the Prophet ﷺ in his life, not just one. He is always in ascension, always with his Lord. He went to the Divine Presence, as God said:
>
> **He was at a distance of two bow-lengths or nearer**[36]
>
> He came very close. "How" is not our business—Allah and the Prophet ﷺ know, because he reached that station. No one can know that level, even Archangel Gabriel ؑ, who accompanied him on all the stages of the Ascension. For when the Prophet ﷺ reached the seventh heaven, Archangel Gabriel ؑ told him, "O Prophet of God, I cannot move further with you. This is my limit. If I go forward, I will be burnt." Despite the Prophet ﷺ telling him to continue with him, Gabriel said, "If I go further, I will be burnt." The Prophet ﷺ then moved alone to the Divine Presence.
>
> The teachings of Naqshbandis and of *awliya*, of Sayyidina Muhyiddin Ibn 'Arabi ق, Sayyidina Abdul-Qadir Jilani ق, and of all the Sufis say that Archangel Gabriel ؑ should have moved forward with the Prophet ﷺ even if he was going to be burnt. As the Prophet ﷺ said to Archangel Gabriel ؑ, "I am going to move even if I am going to be burnt," sacrificing himself to get that light for his Community, with no concern for himself. That is why he

---

[36] Suratu 'n-Najm, 53:9.

was moving forward, constantly progressing, traveling to that level where he came very close to his Lord. At that time God asked him, "Who are you?" What do you think the Prophet ﷺ is going to answer? Is there a "Muhammad" there, is there a "Prophet" there, in the presence of his Lord? Who can be something in the Presence of Allah? So he said, "O my Lord, I am not seeing myself. I am not seeing anything except You. There is no one except You."

That secret is what the Prophet ﷺ wished to pass on to Sayyidina Abu Bakr as-Siddiq ؓ. Thus, he took him to the cave. He could have taken anyone, but he took the one about whom he ﷺ said:

*Whatever my Lord has put in my heart I put in the heart of Abu Bakr as-Siddiq.*

So, as the Prophet ﷺ was lying down, with his head on the leg of Sayyidina Abu Bakr as-Siddiq ؓ, Abu Bakr saw a hole in the wall of the cave and Abu Bakr ؓ put his foot against the hole to close it. He began to feel something biting him and felt great pain. He felt as if he was losing his body. He was trying to control himself, until the flesh of his foot was eaten half away. As his flesh was being eaten, a large snake reared its head. Sayyidina Abu Bakr as-Siddiq ؓ began to cry and a tear fell on the Prophet's ﷺ face. The Prophet ﷺ said, "Oh Abu Bakr! Why are you crying? ***Do not be sad: God is with us!***"[37]

The Prophet's ﷺ question also contains a teaching, because he knows. "Are you afraid," he asked Abu Bakr ؓ, "that people are going to come and kill us?" Abu Bakr ؓ said, "O Messenger of God, I am not crying for fear that they will kill me; I am not afraid of them. But I am crying because of a snake which is eating my foot. When he finishes with me, he will be coming to you, and I

---

[37] Suratu 't-Tawbah, 9:40.

was afraid for you. My heart's blood was burning for you and that is why I cried."

The Prophet ﷺ spoke with the snake and said, "Don't you know that the flesh of prophets is forbidden for you to eat, and the flesh of the veracious saints is also forbidden?" The snake answered, "O Messenger of God, when my Lord created me I knew about you before you were created in this world through your mother's womb, and I asked my Lord forty thousand years ago to keep me alive to see your face and then die. Now Sayyidina Abu Bakr as-Siddiq ؓ is blocking my view with his feet. I have to see you and fulfill my Lord's promise and he is blocking the hole with his feet. That is why I was obliged to eat and come through the hole in order to be able to look at you."

It is reported the Prophet ﷺ said:

*The saliva of a believer is a cure.*[xviii]

That is why you can drink from the same cup, and such is the practice in centers[38] where Sufis come together. One cup is enough, not more, in the modern fashion, which is to have hundreds of cups, and then bring another set of one hundred, wasting money, water, soap, and time because, they say, microbes must not go from one person to another. Where is the belief in the Prophet's ﷺ saying?

Allah is the One who cures and the One who makes you sick, not the cup. If God does not wish you to be sick, even if someone has tuberculosis and you drink after them (a disease quickly spread through drinking) you will not get sick even if you drink hundreds of cups after that person. Allah is ash-Shafi (the Healer), al-Mu'awiy (the Disabler), ad-Darr (the Inflicter). God is the One who alone holds cure and illness in His hands for people.

---

[38] *Zawiya = tekke = dergah*, a Sufi cell or center for retreat or congregation around a shaykh.

So the Prophet ﷺ said, "*Bismillahi 'r-Rahmani 'r-Rahim,*" applied his saliva to the foot of Abu Bakr ؓ, and the foot was immediately healed and whole as before. Then, the Prophet ﷺ ordered the snake to look at him. The snake said, "I believe that there is but One God, and I believe that you are Muhammad ﷺ, His Prophet."

And the snake was coming and turning in circles... Grandshaykh said, according to Sayyidina 'Ali's and Sayyidina Abu Bakr's inspirations, that snake was going around and around for two hours, gazing at the Prophet's ﷺ face. After it looked, the Prophet ﷺ said, "Now what you have asked from your Lord is fulfilled; now, die." That snake died and immediately disappeared. That incident was a test for Sayyidina Abu Bakr as-Siddiq ؓ to see if he was going to protect the Prophet ﷺ or not—was he going to be afraid for himself or for the Prophet ﷺ? But he sacrificed himself for the sake of the Prophet ﷺ.

That was a snake, an animal; what about us? We are not believing, we are denying. To be sure, we are denying. We are believing with our tongues but in our hearts we are denying. We are fighting with one another. And when we fight with each other, that's it! We are denying Allah. We are denying the Prophet ﷺ.

In that sacred, holy cave, God ordered the Prophet ﷺ to pass whatever secrets God had ordered to give, up to a point known to Him, to the heart of Sayyidina Abu Bakr as-Siddiq ؓ. The Prophet ﷺ then passed the secret of his knowledge. That is why this hadith came from Sayyidina Abu Hurayrah ؓ:

> *I have retained from the Prophet ﷺ two vessels of knowledge. One knowledge I have disseminated among people; but if I express the other knowledge, they will cut my throat.*[39]

---

[39] Bukhari.

That is hidden knowledge, *'ilmun min ladunni*.[xix] That knowledge is in the heart only, it can never be written down.[xx] Not everyone can carry this knowledge. That is the knowledge that the Prophet ﷺ put in the heart of Sayyidina Abu Bakr as-Siddiq ؓ.[xxi]

If you look at the Prophetic Traditions (*ahadith*) related on the authority of Sayyidina Abu Bakr as-Siddiq ؓ, you will only see between twenty and thirty. Where is that knowledge that the Prophet ﷺ deposited into his heart? Abu Bakr did not say anything, or so it appears. Do you think he kept that knowledge from people? Whatever the Prophet ﷺ gave him, he has an order to pass on. If he does not pass it on, he betrays the trust that the Prophet ﷺ gave him. The Caliphs of the Prophet ﷺ cannot keep something in their hearts. They have to give; but to give what? To give the knowledge that Sayyidina Abu Hurayrah ؓ described when he said, "If I expressed it, they would cut my throat."

If Sayyidina Abu Bakr as-Siddiq ؓ was going to disseminate that knowledge, Allah knows what they would have said about him—they would have cut his throat. So he hid it. But he passed it on to his successor, Sayyidina Salman al-Farsi ؓ. Then Sayyidina Salman ؓ passed it to Sayyidina Qasim ؓ, the grandson of Sayyidina Abu Bakr ؓ, then Sayyidina Qasim ؓ passed it to Sayyidina Ja'far as-Sadiq ؓ, the Sixth Imam. That secret was passed from one to another, from one to another, from heart to heart, until it reached Mawlana Khalid al-Baghdadi ق. That Golden Chain[40] begins from the Prophet ﷺ, goes to Sayyidina Abu Bakr as-Siddiq ؓ, and then down to Mawlana Khalid al-Baghdadi ق, who is buried in Damascus. Then Mawlana Khalid ق spread it

---

[40] The Golden Chain: the *silsilah* or chain of Khwajagan or spiritual masters of the Naqshbandi-Haqqani Sufi path. This chain culminates with Mawlana Shaykh Muhammad Nazim 'Adil al-Haqqani, who is its fortieth link.

in a huge way between East and West by means of three-hundred deputies (caliphs) so that this knowledge reached everywhere. From Mawlana Khalid ق, that secret was transmitted to the Daghestani line of shaykhs, and traveled from one shaykh to another until it was deposited in the heart of Grandshaykh Abd 'Allah al-Fa'iz ad-Daghestani ق. When he passed from this life, he transmitted that secret to our master, Mawlana Shaykh Nazim ق. That is the origin of the Most Sublime Naqshbandi Order; it began in that cave.

All Sufi orders come from that cave. Someone was reciting the verse of God regarding the Pledge made by the Companions under the tree, before the Treaty of Hudaybiyya:

> **Verily those who pledge their fealty to you (O Muhammad) do no less than pledge their fealty to God: the Hand of God is above their hands: then any one who violates his oath, does so to the harm of his own soul, and any one who fulfils what he has covenanted with God,- God will soon grant him a great Reward.** [41]

This is the open meaning in the Qur'an. The inner meaning, as our Grandshaykh described from his visions during seclusion, is that God ordered the Prophet ﷺ, "O my beloved Muhammad ﷺ, now order all saints to come to your presence." And the Prophet ﷺ immediately ordered Abu Bakr as-Siddiq ؓ and Sayyidina 'Ali ؓ, who was present spiritually, to bring all saints who had taken secrets from Sayyidina 'Ali ؓ or Sayyidina Abu Bakr ؓ to be present in that cave. At that time, 124,000 saints were ready spiritually—even though they had not been created in this world yet; they were present spiritually. And the Prophet ﷺ said to each

---

[41] Suratu 'l-Fath, 48:10.

saint, "Whatever followers you have, whom God gave you on the Day of Promises, call them spiritually."

Everyone was called spiritually to the presence of the Prophet ﷺ in that cave. All of us sitting here, all the Sufi groups wherever they are, it is enough for them to call themselves "Sufi"—they were in the presence of the Prophet ﷺ in that cave. They were present spiritually.

Then God commanded the Prophet ﷺ to order each saint to put his hand over the hand of his disciples to initiate them, and all disciples were putting their hand under the hand of their saints. The Prophet ﷺ ordered Sayyidina 'Ali ؓ to put his hand over all the forty *tariqah* (Sufi paths) that issue from him and ordered Sayyidina Abu Bakr as-Siddiq ؓ to put his hand over the *tariqah* Naqshbandiyyah, the Siddiqiyyah *tariqah*.[42] Then the Prophet ﷺ put his hand over Sayyidina 'Ali ؓ and Sayyidina Abu Bakr as-Siddiq ؓ, and God put His Hand over them and recited that verse Himself:

> ***Those who receive initiation from you receive initiation from God; God's Hand is over their hands; whoever gives back his initiation, he is going to lose; and whoever keeps the promise that he made to God, God will keep that person.***[43]

Immediately, all of us—all forty Sufi paths and the Naqshbandi Path were saying in one sound, with one voice,

ALLAHU ALLAHU ALLAHU HAQQ

ALLAHU ALLAHU ALLAHU HAQQ

ALLAHU ALLAHU ALLAHU HAQQ

---

[42] *Tariqah* – Arabic for the Sufi Path, the method of spiritual progress, the way to the knowledge of God.
[43] Suratu 'l-Fath, 48:10.

... three times, according to God's own wording and all of us were hearing God's own words as that secret was put into our own hearts. After that, Grandshaykh continued, "Anyone who was in that cave was going to be with the others in this life reciting *dhikr*, and anyone who recites *dhikr* must know that he was in the cave with the Prophet ﷺ, with Sayyidina 'Ali ؓ, with Sayyidina Abu Bakr ؓ, and with all the saints."

## Arrival in Madinah

We cannot describe all that happened, but suffice it to know that in that cave a great many secrets were bestowed upon the Sufi people who were following Sayyidina 'Ali ؓ or Sayyidina Abu Bakr as-Siddiq ؓ. And when the Prophet ﷺ continued his migration from Makkah to Madinah, the next day, all of us, the Sufi followers, accompanied the Prophet ﷺ spiritually, migrating with him, from Makkah to Madinah. That is why the People of *Dhikr*, (*adh-dhakireen Allah*), the people of Sufi paths (*al-Qawm*), are with the Prophet ﷺ, migrating from Makkah to Madinah; and that reward is only for the Sufi groups. It is not given to anyone else.

When they reached Madinah, people were watching from the palm-trees in expectation of the Prophet's ﷺ arrival. When those people saw the Prophet ﷺ, accompanied by Sayyidina Abu Bakr as-Siddiq ؓ, and saw the spiritual forms of the people accompanying them, they recited in praise:

> *From the hill-tops of the South,*
> *The full moon doth arise.*
> *With what a lovely call,*
> *Unto God doth he call,*
> *And we thank him for it all,*
> *O you sent by the Merciful,*
> *You have come, best of heralds,*

*You have honored Madinah,
We bow to thy demand.*[44]

They were praising the Prophet ﷺ. As soon as he came to Madinah, he called all his Companions, and then three other secrets were given. We hope to relate them another time.

These secrets concerning the events in that cave were handed on and have come down to us today. This knowledge can never be contained between the two covers of a book. It cannot be written down because fresh knowledge keeps being added to it spontaneously. Still, it is ever the same; yet it is always appropriate to time and place. That is why the order came from Allah in Qur'an:

***O believers, fear God and be with true people***[45]

Because you do not know when they will begin to speak and that secret is revealed. When they speak, that light will come from their speech and you will benefit.

## Bayazid Studies with a Shoemaker

Sayyidina Bayazid al-Bistami ق, one of the Golden Chain in the lineage (*silsilah*) of this Sufi Path (*tariqah*), was a very great and renowned saint. And here in America, they study his teachings wherever Sufism is taught. If I myself say what he used to say, people will call us an unbeliever (*kafir*), because he was sometimes speaking about something on the basis of that secret gnostic knowledge; knowledge which is hidden.

One day Bayazid ق was ordered by his shaykh, "O Bayazid, there is a shoemaker downtown; go and sit with him, and listen to him." What is Sayyidina Bayazid ق, a great gnostic and scholar,

---

[44] From the *Seerah* (Life of the Prophet).
[45] Suratu 't-Tawbah, 9:119.

going to do with a shoemaker? Listen to what? At that time such was his knowledge that everyone knew about him as a learned person (*'alim*) and a gnostic (*'arif*), one who has had experiential knowledge of spiritual realities. But Sayyidina Bayazid ق is not like us.

If our shaykh tells us, "Go and listen to so-and-so," we are going to say, "Me! Listen to *him*? Who is he? He doesn't know anything about Islam, he doesn't know anything about Divine Law (*Shari'ah*), nor about jurisprudence (*fiqh*), and I have to listen to him? No, no, send me to someone else." And if you tell another, "Go and listen to that one," he is going to say, "Am I going to go and listen to that person who knows only Divine Law and jurisprudence? That fundamentalist, fanatic person? No need! We are Sufi, we are free from all that!" So everyone will find an excuse not to listen to the other. Confusion and dissension (*fitna*) come precisely from that. That is why one must say, "God-willing, believers will listen to each other."

How are they going to listen to each other? They will never listen! If you say, "Muslims will fight with each other," I will say yes; but to listen, no, because everyone thinks of himself as having reached the highest level. There is no level above him. Knowledge stops with him! To ask how God sits on the throne[46]— *Astaghfirullah!* (God forgive me)—this is all they know and all they will ever ask. No one wants to understand that:

### *Above each knower there is a higher knower.*[47]

Above every knowledge there is more knowledge. There is no limit to knowledge. What you know, in comparison to the Prophet's ﷺ knowledge and in comparison to God's knowledge, is nothing.

---

[46] cf. Surah Ta Ha, 20:5.
[47] Surah Yusuf, 12:76.

So the order came to listen to a shoemaker, and Bayazid ق, with all his high knowledge both of Divine Law (*Shari'ah*) or external knowledge—and *Haqiqah* or knowledge of the Truth—accepted it because he was humble. He didn't say, "Why?" or "No!" He was following the example of the Prophet ﷺ, who used to wait for Archangel Gabriel ﷺ to come to him and deliver the Message. So Bayazid ق received the order and that was it, "I am going to accept that order and do it."

That shoemaker had been in the vicinity of Sayyidina Bayazid al-Bistami ق for many years, but had veiled himself. So Bayazid had passed by him many times, unaware of his spiritual level, in spite of Bayazid ق being one of the saints of the Golden Chain. For God did not want him to know that one. He was testing him to see if he would listen to him or not. So as he came to the shop, the shoemaker said, "O Bayazid! I've been waiting for you for a long time. Come and sit with me."

## The Spiritual Poles

That shoemaker was the spiritual Pole, *Qutb*, of his time. There are five Pole Saints:

- ❖ Pole of the Lands—Qutbu 'l-Bilad;
- ❖ Pole of Guidance—Qutbu 'l-Irshad;
- ❖ Pole of Poles—Qutbu 'l-Aqtab;
- ❖ Pole of Governance—Qutbu 'l-Mutasarrif and
- ❖ The Greatest Pole—al-Qutbu 'l-'Adham.

Every *qutb* is taking secrets from one prophet of the five great prophets (*uli 'l-'Adham*). The highest *qutb* is taking from the Prophet ﷺ.

For three hours that shoemaker gave a lecture to Sayyidina Bayazid al-Bistami ق. When he finished, Sayyidina Bayazid al-Bistami ق went back to his teaching center and said to his followers, "What I have gained in these three hours and what level I have reached by sitting with this *waliyullah* (Friend of God), I would never have obtained had I worshipped day and night, from the time of Adam ﷺ until the Judgment Day." This is what is referred to in the hadith of the Prophet ﷺ whereby:

> *One hour's reflection is better than seventy year's worship.*[48]

Remembrance, *dhikr*, can be done in many ways: reciting the Names of God, His praise and His glorification, reading Qur'an, praising the Prophet ﷺ, reflecting on what you have done through the day of negative manners or positive manners. All this is considered as Remembrance.[xxii]

Reflection, *tafakkur* or *muraqabah*, however is different. Reflection requires great discipline. To calm the mind, to focus, and to meditate on the object of devotion, and reach a "live" connection therefore, is valued more than years and years of voluntary worship without that light.

God said:

### *O believers, fear God and be with true people*[49]

That is why sitting with true people is very important. Whenever you find a true person, go and sit with him. Even if he does not talk, sit with him. That light in his heart will come to you.[xxiii] There is a saying, "Don't go and sit with the blacksmith, because one ember may fall and burn you; but go and sit with the perfume-maker, because one drop of perfume might fall on you." So when you find such a person, go quickly and sit with him.

---

[48] Ahmad, ad-Darimi, Ibn Majah.
[49] Suratu 't-Tawbah, 9:119.

How do you know a true person? When your heart is quickly connected to him, you must immediately know that this is a true person. If your heart is saying to you, "No, this is not a true person," leave. A true person must be a good example in the community.

Today is the second day of the Islamic month of Muharram al-Haram. It can be considered the Sufi year because it is the date of the migration of Sufi people with the Prophet ﷺ. Next week, on Thursday and Friday, is the tenth of Muharram—the day when the Prophet ﷺ fasted. The tenth of Muharram is when God sent Adam ؈ to earth, and when he saved Noah ؈ (Nuh) from sinking in the ship, saved Abraham ؈ from Nimrod's fire, saved David ؈ (Dawud) and made him to kill Goliath (Jalut), and called Moses ؈ (Musa) to come to Mount Sinai. On that day Jesus ؈ ('Isa) was betrayed; on that day the Prophet ﷺ arrived at Madinah; on that day Sayyidina 'Ali ؆ was killed; on that day the two grandsons of the Prophet ﷺ—through his daughter Fatimah ؆ and her husband 'Ali ؆—Hasan and Husayn ؆ were killed. It is a tremendous day. And so on that day the Prophet ﷺ fasted. Anyone who fasts on that day, that fast will purify him from the sins of the past year and protect him from falling into sins in the new year.[xxiv] Anyone who can fast on that day must know it is a very important day for the folk of our own Sufi path. By God's leave anyone who hears me say this will observe that fast.

Archangel Gabriel ؈ met Khidr ؈ in *dhikr*. Khidr ؈ asked him, "O Gabriel ؈, how long ago did God create Adam ؈?" Archangel Gabriel ؈ answered, "Which Adam are you asking about?" Khidr ؈ said, "Our Adam ؈, my father." Archangel Gabriel ؈ said, "This is the last Adam." Khidr ؈ asked, "Did other Adams pass on this earth?" Archangel Gabriel ؈ answered, "I know that there are 124,000 Adams that came, each with their own generations, each with a Judgment Day, and each with an eternal life. The Adam you mentioned is the last one to be on this earth." Then Khidr ؈ asked, "Has anyone met and accompanied these 124,000 Adams, or were they for their period only?" He answered, "Yes; of the 124,000 saints, every saint is representing one Adam, and the Prophet Muhammad ﷺ was a prophet for all these 124,000 Adams. They were passing one after the other and Muhammad ﷺ was a prophet for each one of them. All 124,000 saints that are on this earth presently, in this last period, have accompanied the Prophet ﷺ with all these Adams, and all their followers were followers of 124,000 Adams—all Sufi people that recite *dhikr* and are following a master who is a real spiritual guide and is one of these 124,000 saints are, in fact, ccompanying the 124,000 Adams."[50]

Mawlana Grandshaykh 'Abd Allah ق and Mawlana Shaykh Nazim ق have said that secret will be revealed for everyone in the time of Mahdi ﷺ. You are going to see this as though you were living it.[xxv] This was given to those people who were in that cave when the Prophet ﷺ migrated from Makkah to Madinah. Anyone present there was in the presence of the 124,000 Adams.

You must be happy, O People of *Dhikr*, for you are connected to a very powerful shaykh! It is not an easy thing. It is a reward from God. He did not ask you about it; He granted it to you. All praise be to our Lord, *Alhamdulillah,* that we have such a connection with our shaykhs.

---

[50] Cf. Ibn al-'Arabi, *Futuhat*, III, 348, 549.

# Advice on Honey

Bees find their way to roses by revelation (*wahy*) from God. That is why God says in the Qur'an that in honey is a cure from diseases for humankind because it is revealed to bees which flowers to visit and from which to take that healing.

> *And your Lord revealed to the Bee to ...find with skill the spacious paths of its Lord: there issues from within their bodies a drink of varying colours, wherein is healing for humankind...* [51]

Is it not true that for everything one loves, one expresses that love using the language of flowers? Flowers mean love, but honey is love too. That is why we hear people speak of their "honeymoon." By virtue of love everything lives and has being. It is a cure for human beings. The Prophet ﷺ, since there was no tea in his time, used to make hot water and put one spoonful of honey in it early in the morning. It is a cure for at least seventy diseases. Use honey and you will be cured from your sicknesses, by the Will of God.

---

[51] Suratu 'l-Isra, 17:68,69.

## MIRACLES IN THE NAQSHBANDI WAY

In the Naqshbandi Sufi order one does not have permission to display miraculous powers. In the other forty Sufi orders, you have permission to show all manner of miraculous powers although it will not bring you to a higher standard.[xxvi] Grandshaykh was ordered by his shaykh to "divorce" miraculous powers. He used to possess and display miracles excessively. Then his shaykh said, "As they divorce a woman from a man, you must divorce miraculous powers; don't return to them—there is no need. People have to follow us because of our inspired knowledge (*'ilm*)—not because we can go through the wall, walk on fire, or fly in the skies." I know many shaykhs who take this [holds his belt to his ear], and they speak through it like a telephone. Then they call your parents in their country, just like this. This is not something we like in the Naqshbandi order.

I will tell you a story of Sayyidina Shah Naqshband, the leader of this order. In those days in Bukhara, they used to harvest wheat, grind it to flower, and make bread to eat. There occurred a drought in the land, and for two or three years there was no rain. So there were no crops, and, therefore no flour in the city. Children were dying of hunger. They knew that Shah Naqshband ق was a very great saint, so they came to him saying, "Please help! The whole city is dying." Shah Naqshband ق was renowned for both the external knowledge and the internal knowledge of the faith, and is still considered one of the greatest scholars in Islam.

After seeing the people starving, feelings of compassion overwhelmed his heart. Shah Naqshband ق said, "Whatever wheat remains in the city, bring it to me." They found a small quantity of wheat in the house of the city's wealthiest citizen. They brought that precious wheat to the saint. He went to the flour-mill. At that time they used cows to turn the grinding-stone. So he put that wheat between the two stones, and he put his head in the yoke instead of the cows, and he started going around. As he was turning, flour began to pour out of the mill. The more he walked, the more flour poured forth, and he ordered all the city to come and fill their flour bags. From that small amount of wheat they had brought to him every household filled their flour bags and they had provisions for three or four years ahead. He displayed that miraculous power—but he had displayed it without permission.

Before saints show any miraculous power, they must ask permission from the Prophet ﷺ. If he gives them permission, they can display such power without being blamed for it later. If the Prophet ﷺ does not give permission, then the saint is obliged to keep himself as an ordinary person and not display any difference from common people. Shah Naqshband, although he was the greatest leader in that realm, had not taken permission.

When he was dying, after his disciples had placed him on his bed, they saw him keep falling down. Each time he fell down from his bed—his long beard reaching down—he would repeat, "Ya 'Afuww ya 'Afuww... O Forgiver, forgive me, O Forgiver, forgive me...," and kept crying. God spoke to him through his heart asking him, "Why did you show miraculous powers? Do you have more mercy in your heart than I? Didn't I know that they were starving? I am the One who made them starve. Why did you interfere with My Will?"

Great saints know that if you display miraculous powers, you are interfering with God's Will. That is why they do not like to show them. They want to keep swimming in that ocean, and, whatever of His Will God has written to come to pass, they accept and do not attempt to change. Saints of a lesser level attempt to change the Will of God because they have not yet arrived at that stage of perfection. That is why Naqshbandi shaykhs, who hold their secrets from the Prophet ﷺ, do not display miraculous powers. Their miraculous power consists only in their knowledge, the inspirations that come to their hearts. They do not try to show physical miracles.

I know of a saint in Tripoli, Lebanon. It is a very famous story my father and my uncles often tell. His name is Shaykh 'Ali al-'Omari, a Qadiri saint. An Italian ship came to the Lebanese shore in 1942. That ship was full of food packages for the Lebanese people, but for some reason, the Italian commander refused to unload the ship, saying he had orders to return. That saint went to the seashore, took a fishing-pole, hooked the ship and held it, just like that, and the ship could not move—finished. He said, "I will not let the ship move until they unload its cargo." After two or three days of negotiations he was still there, without need for him to go to make ablution, eat, or other normal needs. He would pray while holding his fishing-pole. He would not move. When they had finally unloaded the ship, he released it.

## Saints are Alive in Their Graves

There are saints who interfere. But this does not characterize the highest level of perfection. There was a Naqshbandi saint by the name of Sa'd ad-Din Jabawi. When I was about eighteen or nineteen years old I saw a tremendous event concerning him. I was in Grandshaykh's house in Damascus. A delegation of scholars visited him, saying, "O Mawlana, they want to make a road, and Sidi Sa'd ad-Din Jabawi's shrine (*maqam*), is in the way. The government sent bulldozers to raze that grave, but they cannot touch it. Every time the bulldozer comes to that point, it stops. If they try to strike the grave, the bulldozer breaks down." They had come to Grandshaykh knowing there is connection with Sidi Sa'd ad-Din Jabawi through the Naqshbandi Sufi order, and asked him, "Please, solve this problem for us." Mawlana Shaykh

'Abd Allah replied, "Give me two or three days." After two days, he said, "Go to the place of that saint tonight; make *dhikr*, all of you together; then open his grave in the morning, and remove him for burial elsewhere."

But Sidi Sa'd ad-Din Jabawi had died five hundred years ago! So they said like the Wahhabis say today, "What is left of him?" They said, "He's finished; there's just dust there now!" What dust? The Prophet ﷺ said:

> *God has forbidden the earth to eat the body of prophets.*[52]

God has said in Qur'an:

> **They (martyrs) are alive in the presence of their Lord, being provided for.**[53]

What is true of prophets and martyrs in these two examples is true of saints also, of righteous people, of true people. They are alive. So those scholars were laughing, saying, "Is he still there?" Of course, they should have known he was still there, otherwise, why was the bulldozer unable to go through? That night they went and made *dhikr* as a group. In the morning, Shaykh 'Abd Allah's students began to open the grave—block after block—until they came to the main stone. They took that big stone away and the air all around was diffused with a beautiful fragrance. A brilliant light emerged. It was the hour of the dawn prayer (Fajr), when all is dark, with the day just beginning to break on the horizon. They found the saint there in his burial shroud, as though he had been buried that very day, perfectly clean, his face looking as if he had just died. It seemed as if his skin would redden if you just pinched it. I was there. When they opened the tomb and

---

[52] Ahmad, Abu Dawud, Ibn Abi Shaybah, Nasa'i, Ibn Majah, ad-Darimi, Ibn Khuzaymah, Hakim, adh-Dhahabi, at-Tabarani, Bayhaqi.
[53] Surat Ali-'Imran, 3:169.

removed him I was with my brother. They lifted him from the grave, and buried him in another place not far away.

He had been buried there for five-hundred years. What is this saying by some so-called scholars that "there are no saints," when God says in His Holy Qur'an:

> **God's saints—there is no fear and no sadness for them**[54]

and in a Divine Saying:

> My saints are under My domes, no one knows them other than Myself.[55]

Scholars are known by everyone. If our Lord wanted to mention scholars in this statement He would have said "My scholars" (*'ulama'ee*). But He said, "My *saints* (*awliya'ee*) are under My domes," not, "My *scholars* are under My domes." No one knows them—they are hidden. You cannot buy sanctity with a scholar's knowledge (*'ilm*). Sainthood is granted to people by God. Saints do not become saints by going to universities and receiving degrees. The condition of sainthood is a reward granted from God to a person's heart. Even if he knows nothing at all in the way of academic knowledge, God opens up paths in his heart, and, at that time, there is nothing he does not know.[xxvii]

## Seek a Saint and You Will Find One

If anyone looks for a saint, he will find one. If anyone looks for a scholar, *'alim*, he will find one. If anyone looks for a person of character he will find one, and if anyone searches out a corrupt person, he will find one. Whatever the intention of your heart is, you will find what is in accord with it.[xxviii] If your intention is to be

---

[54] Suratu 'l-Anbiya, 10:62.
[55] *Hadith qudsi*, Ghazali, Hujwiri.

with a saint, you are going to find a saint, for who put that intention in your heart? God did. He is telling you, "Look for My saintly ones." If your intention is to find a scholar (*'alim*), you will find one, and if your intention is to find a sincere, righteous person, you will find one.

One day when I was a young boy, around the year 1955, I was with my oldest brother, who was about twenty-five at the time, in the Grand Mosque of Beirut. It was the time for the afternoon prayer (Salat al-'Asr), and my uncle, who was the mufti, was leading the prayer. A person with a jet-black beard entered the mosque, and came and sat next to my brother. The afternoon prayer was ending.

My brother had been looking for saints since childhood. We were connected on my uncle's side to Shaykh Muhammad Amin al-Kurdi ق in Egypt, and to Shaykh Ibrahim Ghalayini ق, in Damascus. The person who sat beside him was very handsome, with striking blue eyes, a white complexion, and a wearing a turban. He called my brother saying, "Are you Salim?" My brother answered, "Yes, how do you know me?" He said, "Don't ask—you are Naqshbandi?" My brother said, "Yes." He continued, "You are in a branch of Naqshbandi; you are not in the main trunk." He said, "I have been sent to you by my master, Shaykh 'Abd Allah, from Damascus. It is time for you to go and meet him." That was Shaykh Nazim. I was then ten years old.

When your heart is looking for a saint, you will find him, and your heart will tell you "this is a saint." Your ego, however, will come and say "No!", and interrupt you. When this happens, know that you are on the right way. Sometimes you will think, "This is a saint," and then, "This is not a saint." At that time, you must know that there is a reality there.

We were attracted to Shaykh Nazim. We loved him because there was light coming from him. My brother took him to meet my uncle, and we then invited him to our house. He stayed overnight. The next day he told us, "Come with me to Damascus."

We went to Damascus. *Subhanallah!* When we saw Grandshaykh 'Abd Allah, we felt a tremendous attraction. We saw that all shaykhs in Syria were coming to him, yet Grandshaykh did not know how to read or write. Big scholars with big turbans next to which ours are small, people seventy and eighty years of age, came and sat like children in front of Grandshaykh. And when Grandshaykh opened his advice, their learning was as nothing. They found something extraordinary. He gave explanations that no one had heard before. We were so attracted that from that time until now, thank God, *Alhamdulillah,* that early connection is still there.

Saints come to you; but they come once. If you do not catch them, they do not come a second time. You have to be very careful. They are not like scholars. Scholars even go from door to door. In Montreal, they take the Muslims names out of directories; missionary Muslims who come knocking at people's doors! Scholars like to run after people to bring them to their classes because they have nothing to give. But saints have everything, and therefore, you need come only one time—then you are connected. That's it. Then they leave you. Whenever they want you, they pull that rope back and you will return to their presence. One minute of sitting in their association is enough to be taken with them on the Judgment Day. But everyone must be aware of this fact:

Saints come one time, not twice. They do not like to insist. If you take the opportunity, and attach yourself to them, that's it. If you lose that opportunity, you lose them in this life, but not in the hereafter. When you have sat with them once, it is enough for you; but in this life, you will not feel the great happiness, nor see the spiritual progress that comes with accompanying such saints.

Do not allow too many doubts to enter into your mind; do not cause your heart to shake and become unsteady. They are not asking anything from anyone. They work only for Allah. If anyone believes, he will benefit. If anyone disbelieves, he is the loser. They are not telling everyone to come and believe in them.

People ask Mawlana Shaykh Nazim, "Why are you not going after people to make them come to the Way?" He says:

> What God sends, these are selected people. We don't want the unselected. There are many people outside. You can go to them. I am leaving them for others. I want the selected ones. When the selected ones come, you can depend on them. The unselected ones come and go, come and go, like a sieve. Then, you throw out what is left. What remains are the selected ones.

Saints need select people. They do not want the "leftovers." I do not mean "leftovers" with respect to people's hearts but with respect to their moral character. Saints, then, take what comes to them. What is left, is discarded. Do not lose that opportunity and be like something discarded. Reality does not visit people many times in this life. In fact, it comes only once.

## Belief in the Unseen

As Qur'an said:

***Those who believe in the unseen...***[56]

You have to have faith in the Unseen. That is why the Sufi teachers of the Naqshbandiyyah order do not like to show miracles. If I pass through this wall to the other side, you are certainly going to believe. But what is the value of that belief—nothing at all. That is why the first pillar of religion in Islam is

---

[56] Suratu 'l-Baqara, 2:3.

faith in the Unseen. If you want to see, then there is no faith: you have seen. Your spiritual standing, therefore, will not be high.

What made the Companions of the Prophet ﷺ become Companions and achieve that high level? It is because they believed in the Unseen. The Prophet ﷺ came, and everyone was worshipping idols. He said, "Leave idols and worship God!" Idolaters said, "But where is God—we are not seeing God, but we see the idols?" Those who accepted the Prophet's ﷺ teachings believed in the Unseen and became his Companions. Therefore the Companions believed in the Unseen. Once they believed, God sent more to their hearts. That is why He said to them in Qur'an:

### *O believers, believe in God and in His Prophet.* [57]

"*O believers...*" He called them believers, because they believed in the Unseen. Previously they were unbelievers; He called them to believe in the Unseen, to believe in Him. When they said, "Yes, we believe," He called them believers: believers, but without seeing. Now, He wants to raise them. He is going to take them from the "unseen" position to the "seen" position.

"*O believers, believe!...*" If they were called believers to start with, what is left to believe in? Why is He ordering them again to believe? This means that the initial belief referred to at the beginning of the verse was a lower level—imitative belief. He wants to raise them, "Believe now, in God and His Apostle." It means, "I am going to show you that light in your hearts. I am raising you from the level of imitation, which is the common level for everyone, to the level of seeing, the heart level which is higher—belief in God and in the Prophet ﷺ."[xxix] Though they believed already, He wants to show them a higher level.

---

[57] Suratu 'n-Nisa, 4:136.

Now, our belief is mere imitation. Our ego is fighting us—"No, he is not right; yes, he is right... Don't accept this; accept that..." When we accept, they will take you to the other shore. What do you need in order to cross that ocean from this shore to that? You need the means: a bridge or a vehicle to take you, such as a ship or an airplane. If you do not find that means, you will never reach the farther shore. This is why God gave this order, *"O believers, believe!..."* in Qur'an. They were believers in the Unseen on this shore, having been accepted by Him; but He wants to take them to the second shore, and He told them *"Believe"* yet again, in God and His Prophet ﷺ, so they can cross to the shore of safety.

## Levels in the Naqshbandi Order

There are three levels in the Naqshbandi order:

- ❖ The Knowledge of Certainty—*Ilmu 'l-Yaqeen*;
- ❖ The Eye of Certainty—*'Aynu 'l-Yaqeen*;
- ❖ The Truth of Certainty—*Haqqu 'l-Yaqeen*.

But prior to reaching this level of understanding, you must have reached three other levels:

- ❖ Love of God, *Mahabbatullah*;
- ❖ Love of the Prophet ﷺ, *Mahabbatu 'l-habib*;
- ❖ Love of the saints, *Mahabbatu 'l-mashayikh*.

When you love a woman, she is always present in your heart. You are always seeing her. When you love someone, you are always remembering her either over the phone, buying her roses or taking her on a picnic. Look what happened to Romeo and Juliet, how Romeo spent all his nights either with his guitar or his poetry, she up on the balcony, and he sending poems up to her—remembering her.

The first level in Sufism—and in Divine Law *(Shari'ah)* also, it is the same in both—is love of God. If you do not have love for

Allah, how are you going to find true pleasure? Everyone in this life now has love for the world (*dunya*), but not for Allah. We all have love for the material world. Everyone wants to get what they can from this worldly life. Don't they know that Allah, who created this world, has everything?

They say in Arabic, *ma si-wallah*—"whatever is other than God." There is God, and there is what God created. They are seeking the created, they are not seeking the Creator. People chase whatever is other than God—the material world. But who created that material world? Is not God its Creator? And if His name is "the Creator," it means every moment He is creating something. His creation does not cease. Do you want to run after such a Creator who has everything and keeps creating, or do you want to run after some superficial invention made by human beings?

Now in our countries anyone who runs after religion seeking reality is called a "backward" person (*raj'i*). In all Arab countries and all Muslim countries without exception, anyone who seeks reality, who seeks God, who seeks love, is called regressive.

Is someone who seeks His Lord "backwards"? This is the attitude now in those regions. They look at you wondering, "what kind of people are these?" They are ashamed of you in their society. We are not saying this to be fundamentalist, but we say it to be good people; people with positive manners in society, loving God, loving the Prophets, loving saints, loving humble people.

What is the shame in this? Everyone is running after the pleasures of this life. No one is running after the Creator of pleasures, the One who has everything. I remember Grandshaykh once sitting and speaking about Mahdi ﷺ He said, "Men are running after women, and women are running after men. And all the focus of human mentality is this—sexuality; there is nothing else! Everyone is running after that, they have that intention in mind. Yet, that intention is coming from God's Ocean of Beauty. God has created that beauty within both men and women."

We are not saying that this love of beauty and physical attraction is forbidden. God has permitted human beings to love that beauty. Grandshaykh said, "In the time of Mahdi's ﷺ, when Mahdi ﷺ opens the light of that Ocean to every man and every woman, by God's permission; and when they look at that Ocean of Beauty God is sending them, the thought of sexual relations will be as nothing—as spit—because you will have the whole ocean of pleasure."

This is what God mentioned in the Qur'an and the Prophet ﷺ said in hadith: in Paradise you are always in never-ending, continuous pleasure. Now, you take your pleasure for one hour—then it is over. There, it is continuous, for men and for women. When Mahdi ﷺ opens that Ocean, everyone is going to be running after the light coming from it: the light of complete love.

Now we are trading with God because we do not see. When we are able to see, in Mahdi's ﷺ time, there will be no more trading. Traders are trading now—those that are trying to hold themselves in order not to fall into the pleasures of this life. Whoever falls into the pleasures of this life now, will not find himself in a high spiritual rank in Mahdi's ﷺ time. The Prophet ﷺ said:

> *Anyone who grasps his religion firmly and faithfully will be like one grasping a burning ember.*[58]

Anyone that tries to hold himself now, is going to get everything later. But if you allow your body to take everything from this life now, you are not going to find happiness and pleasure at that time.

---

[58] Tirmidhi, Ahmad, al-Hakim.

The first stage, as we said, is love of God, love of the Prophet ﷺ and love of saints. When you have that love, they are always present in your heart. Then you will reach:

- ❖ The Presence of God—*Hudurullah,*
- ❖ The Presence of the Prophet ﷺ—*Huduru 'l-Habib;*
- ❖ The Presence of the saints—*Huduru 'l-mashayikh.*

When you have presence, you do not feel anything present except God at that time. Then you have:

- ❖ Annihilation in God—*Fana'un fillah,*
- ❖ Annihilation in the Prophet ﷺ—*Fana'un fi 'r-rasul,*
- ❖ Annihilation in the saints—*Fana'un fi 'l-mashayikh.*

At that time you vanish into the stage of non-existence. You are non-existent, while God exists; the Prophet ﷺ exists; your shaykh exists. Through your shaykh you go to the Prophet ﷺ, and then your shaykh vanishes. Then, the Prophet ﷺ hands you over to the Divine Presence.

## Three Levels of Knowledge

When you have accomplished those three levels of annihilation, only then you go to:

- ❖ The Knowledge of Certainty—*'Ilmu 'l-Yaqeen,*
- ❖ The Vision of Certainty—*'Aynu 'l-Yaqeen,*
- ❖ The Reality of Certainty—*Haqqu 'l-Yaqeen,*

the three levels of certainty that we began mentioning above.

Right now you may have a level of certainty, you may know it, having heard and understood something about those Oceans of Beauty, but you cannot feel it, see it or experience it. As we are discussing what Mahdi ﷺ is going to open from the Oceans of Beauty, you are hearing, taking knowledge from that, while some of you are sensing it. The second level, the Vision of Certainty, *'Aynu 'l-Yaqeen*, is when you can see. When Mawlana Shaykh Nazim speaks, you can see that light; but you cannot feel it, you cannot take the pleasure. The Reality of Certainty, *Haqqu 'l-Yaqeen* is the level where you hear, see and feel.

The first knowledge is through hearing. That is why in all verses in the Qur'an where God wants to begin describing humankind's faculties, He first says "hearing"—everything begins with hearing. At the second level you can both see and hear without feeling, like television: you can see and hear the speaker, but you cannot feel as if you were sitting with him. The third level is as if you are sitting with them in the studio, feeling everything. When present, past, and future events are mentioned you will experience them. When you are with saints at that level, you will see all three realms.

This is what the Prophet ﷺ told the Companions ؓ when he ordered, "Come to me and come to Allah." That is why God told them this verse in the Holy Qur'an:

### *O believers, believe...*[59]

His taking them from the position of "belief—unseen" to the position of "belief—seen" hinges on the command "Believe!"

That kind of higher belief they did not have, but they had what can be called imitative belief—the position of belief in the Unseen. What the Prophet ﷺ meant is, "I want you now to see and to feel what you used only to hear"—the second and third levels: the Vision of Certainty, and the Reality of Certainty.

The Prophet ﷺ took the believers from one shore of the ocean to the other shore with God's command to believe. He showed them complete feelings of happiness and perfect pleasure. If all of

---

[59] Suratu 'n-Nisa, 4:136.

us direct ourselves to God and the Prophet ﷺ and put the love of God and His Prophet in our hearts, at that time they will take us from the level of believing in the Unseen—which is mere imitation—to a level of real belief because it is belief in the Seen.

This is what Naqshbandi teachings strive to show—to take you from the Unseen to the Seen: feeling and seeing. Now Muslim people worship five times a day, according to Divine Law (*Shari'ah*), beginning with the words "God is greater! *Allahu Akbar...*" and praying. But if your heart is preoccupied with materialism and busy with the world of material you are still standing in the Unseen position. If you go higher, these teachings will take you from the Unseen to the Seen, and when you say "God is greater! *Allahu Akbar*," you will find yourself standing before the Ka'bah, seeing and feeling yourself praying there.

The first level is obedience to the Divine Law (*Shari'ah*), while the next level is the Path, *Tariqah*. The Divine Law is the ocean while the Path is the ship, the means that allows you to cross that ocean. It will protect you from sinking. It will make you see, because it polishes you, scrubbing the rust from your heart. God willing, all of us will be following the truth and not accepting what our ego is telling us. We are not telling you not to take your share from this life. Take your share from this life, but while you place one foot here in this world place the other foot in the Hereafter.

# SWIMMING IN YOUR ORBIT

*A believer keeps his promise...*[60]

You find a lot of this in America and western countries. If you ask an American to promise something, and he says "yes," then that is it! He will not change, whatever happens. There may be exceptions, but the majority will not change. This is what I saw here. In the Far East and the Middle East, a person will abandon his promise one hundred times, not just once! Every moment, he will change.

Even sincere people, who genuinely attempt to conform their character to the teachings of the Prophet ﷺ and the teachings of the Sufis, do not keep their promises; yet Westerners do. On the Day of Promises, when we promised God to worship Him, and declared, "You are our Lord and we are Your servants," we accepted a solemn covenant. When we came to this earth, we denied our oath. All of us denied it. That is why God said:

> **We have offered the heavens, the earth, and the mountains Our Trust to carry, but they were unable to carry it and were afraid; and humans accepted it—indeed he was unjust and ignorant.**[61]

Humans were tyrants to themselves in accepting to carry this trust because, when you accept something as a trust, you have to return it; if you are not going to return it, you show ignorance in having accepted it. On the Day of Promises we accepted our Lord.

---

[60] Abu Dawud, Ahmad, Daraqutni, Al-Hakim.
[61] Suratu 'l-Ahzab, 33:72.

Now, when we come here, we run away. We are saying "no" to what Moses ﷺ said, "no" to what Jesus ﷺ said, and "no" to what Prophet Muhammad ﷺ said; "no" to being a benefit to society. "This is backward. It is nonsense. Tend to the material side of life! Take your pleasure! Be an atheist! Don't accept any teachings about good character and manners."

This is what they tell people. On television they are teaching people negative habits and character. Many say, "We don't like televisions in our house." Why? Is it not a modern invention? Why do you dislike it? "Because," they say, "it will ruin our children." This is true. But if everyone knows something will ruin their children, why is it being broadcast on hundreds of stations?

## God Defends His House

When Abraha, a great king, came to destroy the House of God, the Ka'bah, in Makkah, the heads of the tribes came to 'Abd al-Muttalib, the Prophet's grandfather—who was in charge of looking after Ka'bah before the Prophet's ﷺ coming. They said to him, "Abraha is coming with his armies to destroy the Ka'bah!" He said, "I don't care. I have to care for my own house; as for God's House, God has to take care of it." What did God send? He sent small birds carrying pebbles, with which they pelted Abraha's army. As soon as a stone would hit someone, that person died, as recompense for his tyranny.

Now, people are tyrants on themselves. They are teaching children sex on television. I remember that Mawlana Shaykh Nazim said in 1976, "God is sending a disease that no one will be able to face." No one had heard about AIDS in 1976—it appeared in the eighties. Now everyone is afraid.

God has given you a trust to keep in your heart. You have to return it. If you lose it, He is going to ask you where you lost it. If you have a good excuse at that time, it is alright, He will excuse you. But if you don't give a good excuse... think of what you are going to say to Him at that time. Do you know what you are going to say? I will tell you. (Now, I am going to say something, which when people read it, will make them cry out and object.)

God has created everything with love. Because of this, He will also save everything with love. He knows that we are ignorant. He mentioned it when He said:

> **But humanity undertook [the Trust]; He was indeed unjust and foolish**[62]

## God is not a Torturer

God knows our weakness and ignorance, and since He knows, He has to create something to save us. And there are many ways, many means to save human beings. Do you think God created us with His own Hands, with love, lovingly kneading us like dough, to throw that object of His love into Hell, to burn it up and look at it with happy detachment?

Today they build fireplaces inside houses, and he [pointing to a disciple], is happy with fire. Just the other day, he installed a big stove in his basement and now he goes down every hour and stuffs wood inside it: day and night. Once his wife forgot to put wood in the stove, so he was shouting at her like a madman! Is God going to put us in hell, like him putting wood in his stove, one after another, and to burn us up saying, "To Hell, move, and more besides, to make a big fire!"?

## Saints Move Everywhere

God is merciful with His servants. He created ways to save them from punishment, by sending messengers and prophets to guide the human race towards their eternal life. Everyone will be judged at that time according to their intentions. Those who have

---

[62] Suratu 'l-Ahzab, 33:72.

positive intentions and their actions were commendable, will have a happy eternal life; those who did not will be under the mercy of their Lord.

There are many ways that God has created and given as power into the hands of messengers, prophets and their inheritors, the saints, to bring human beings to the shore of safety. That is why this earth will never be empty of saints, never! There are 124,000 saints in every century. When one dies, another must replace him and sit in his "chair." There is no place, even if you are on a mountain making seclusion, except there is an order for a saint to pass there at least once every three days, to look at you and go. No one is left on this earth in twenty-four hours or three days except one of these 124,000 saints will pass by, look at him and carry his burdens for him. They are all covering this earth.

Within the 124,000 there are five groups of special saints: *Budala, Nujaba, Nuqaba, Awtad, Akhyar*. Every one of these groups counts seven-hundred saints. These five groups total 3500 saints from the 124,000. From among them are more select ones, and so on, in an hierarchy. For everyone, through God's mercy and love, there is a means to find a way to God. That is why the Prophet ﷺ said:

> *The ways to God are as numerous as the breaths of human beings.*[63]

There are many ways to God; thousands, millions, rather an infinite number of ways. If you find your way, follow it. When you follow it, do not then go to another way. If you know that this

---

[63] See Najmuddin al-Kubra, *Al-usul al-'ashra*, ed. Merijan Mole, in *Annales Islamologiques* vol. IV (1963) p. 15; also Sulami's *Tabaqat as-sufiyah* (ed. Cairo, 1969) p. 383 (Abul Hasan al-Muzayyin, "Ways to God number as the stars") and p. 472 (Abu Bakr at-Tamistani, "Ways to God number as human beings").

is the highest way, hold it tight and keep it. *Insha-Allah*, you will find your safety, the ship that carries you:

### *each one swimming in his orbit.* [64]

This refers to the stars. Are there no orbits for human beings? You have an orbit; I have an orbit; he has an orbit. Everyone is swimming in his orbit. You cannot come to my orbit, I cannot go to his orbit. What is that orbit? Where are you swimming? The mind thinks, then the heart is inspired. Where are we swimming? We are not seeing anything except our bodies and we are sitting here. Open the eyes, open the ears of your hearts, and you will find yourself and know where you are swimming.

## Use What God Gave You!

Human beings today are inventing microchips and making gadgets like this [pointing to a tape recorder]. It hears and records everything. Why are you not recording here [points to his chest]? Why are you not seeing here? Because you are not using the means God gave you. Use it!

### *O human beings and jinn! If you are able to penetrate through the orbits of heaven and earth, penetrate, go! But you cannot do so unless you have the means.* [65]

God is showing you the way, saying, "take a means" to go through that orbit. People invent means. They sent Columbia [a space shuttle] into space, circling the planet, even now. Spiritually also, there are many space shuttles to take you round your orbit. You have to choose the means, the right means—where is that

---

[64] Surah Ya Sin, 36:40.
[65] Suratu 'r-Rahman, 55:33.

means? Find it. And if you find that saint who will take you into your orbit, then you can swim.

That means is a secret code. Nowadays, they put a plastic card into the slot at the door of a building and the door opens. Why? Because there is a secret code there. What is your secret code in order to enter and swim in your orbit? Do you know it? If you find it, you can open and see what is inside. If you do not find it, you cannot swim in that orbit. You are still swimming in your cage. Find that plastic card. Plug it in. Immediately, the door will open for you, and you are everywhere, swimming. There is nothing closed to you at that time. But everyone is running after the pleasures of this life. Very few people say, "I am finished with it," and direct their hearts towards Allah Sublime and Exalted.

## God's Favors: Either Earned or Granted

This is a grant from God. To whomever God grants that title, he or she will quickly find that plastic card. It is ready. People are two kinds: either taking it as a favour granted by God (*wahban*), without asking for it; or having to work in order to acquire it (*kasban*). So try to work and acquire it. Only saints take it without asking for it. Others have to work and work for it in order to get it. God willing, it is not far from any one of us. You are very near reality. It needs some more steps, some more seeking of the right ways, and you are going to find it near you.

## Don't Surrender Like a Corpse

Some people come to Mawlana Shaykh Nazim as sinners, sit with him for one hour, then go out again as saints. Some people enter as mere worshippers and leave in the same way. Because they do not come with complete *taslimiyya*, surrendering. If you do not surrender, you are never going to find reality. You have to make a complete surrender. Shah Naqshband ق said, "I do not like for my disciple (*murid*) to surrender to me like a dead person." How is surrendering done then? That person is surrendering completely, he cannot do anything. He said no, this is still not good enough, because if you wash that corpse with cold water, he is saying, "This is cold water." If you wash him with hot water, he will say, "This is hot water," for if you push his hand back and forth a little bit, he can feel (when God takes out the spirit he leaves one part there for Judgment Day, so that the dead person knows himself to be present there).

So Shah Naqshband ق said he did not like the dead person's kind of surrender, because a dead person still has a will. They asked him, "Then what kind of surrender do you ask of us?"

Shah Naqshband ق said:

I want a surrender like that of a tree-leaf when it dries up, dies and is ready to fall to the ground, and the wind will bear it off the branch and carry it north, south, east or west but it will not say anything. Wherever the wind takes it, it will go. No will; no partial will; nothing! Surrendering to the will of God. If the wind later takes it to a fireplace, it will go there also, and it will burn. I want a surrender like that from my disciple. At that time, I will open the door for him.

We are not surrendering. We are surrendering to our ego. Whatever our ego asks from us, we are doing. Whatever God is asking us, we are not accepting. That is why we are still one foot in *"then they believe"* (*thumma amanu*) and one foot in *"then they disbelieve"* (*thumma kafaru*).[66] We are this way, then that way. Even if you go *"then they believe"* (*thumma amanu*)—as believers—for ninety-nine feet, if the last foot, the one-hundreth footstep is *"then they disbelieve"* (*thumma kafaru*), coming as an unbeliever, you will lose everything and must return all the way back to the first step. You will fall: what you have gained, you now lose; now begin

---

[66] Suratu 'n-Nisa, 4:137.

again. Therefore be very careful not to fall. Try always to be climbing, as a believer, with a good heart, forgiving, forgiving, forgiving, making peace, forgetting. Then you will find yourself approaching. If you do not do that, then it will be very difficult to be on this path—to be a select person. If you want to be a selected person who seeks reality, you have to always be good, you cannot be up one day, down the next. That is for common people. Selected people must always be going up.

## Help Others, for God's Sake

There are many ways to be constructive, always helping people. God asked Moses , "O Moses, what are you doing for Me?" He said, "O my Lord, I am praying to You, always worshipping You." God said, "No, your worship is for you; what are you doing for Me?" He said, "My Lord, what can I do for You? Tell me." God said, "Help My servants. If you help them, then you are doing something for Me." So, if we find that our brothers and sisters need help, we have to help. Then, we will be going up quickly.

## The Necessity for Guidance

God said in the Holy Qur'an:

*Which then is best?—he that layeth his foundation on piety to Allah and His good pleasure?—or he that layeth his foundation on an undermined sand-cliff ready to crumble to pieces?*[67]

If someone lays the foundation of his house on solid ground, piece by piece, well placed, then he will find his house is well-built. But for every thing you need an expert. If I say to our brother, "Can you build a house for us?" He will say, "No, I am not a carpenter." So we are obliged to call another one and say, "Please, build a house for us, because you are an expert." And he will tell you, "Alright, this is the plan, here we put that wall, here the foundation, here cement," and so forth.

If you need an expert for an ordinary house, how about your heart? How do you approach your Lord without an expert? You have to look for an expert. You cannot reach without one, as much as you are going to try to move in this path alone. No one, by himself, can reach because, sometimes, even though he knows he is on the right path, he might build something not in its place; then it will fall. So we need an expert, and that expert is our guide.

Guidance is important. If you do not have a guide to guide you where to go, then you are going to find many difficulties in your way. When you go into a desert, they tell you beware, do not

---

[67] Suratu 't-Tawbah, 9:109.

go into that desert because you are going to suffer. They might show you the beginning of the way, nevertheless, you need a guide to show you the rest of the way through the desert. Why is this? Because in the desert everything looks the same, and when winds come, the sand changes its place, and then you do not know which way is the right one. An expert, a guide, even if the winds come, can take you along the right way. And in two or three days you have passed through the desert and reached the other side.

## Criteria of the True Guide

Also, to reach your Lord, you can never find your way through the desert except with a guide (*daleel*), because the wind of the ego changes everything, *al-hawa,* in Arabic—desires, vain passions. The ego has desires, and the wind of the ego is nothing but empty desires and vain passions. When desires overcome your ego, they veil the right path for you; then you are lost, you are going to stop and not know how to continue. That is why you need a guide who is an expert in the ways of the desert. He is an expert in the roads that traverse the ego.

If you cannot find such a guide, then you are wasting your time in reaching your Lord in this life. But God is merciful. Because you are trying to reach, you will reach at the end, even without a guide; but you will not reach quickly. Now you are losing time, not progressing... But as soon as you find that guide and you accept him to show you the shortcut through the desires of the ego, through the will of the ego, which is vain passion and desire, then you are going to find yourself on the safe shore. Otherwise you will be lost in that vast desert.

When the Prophet ﷺ was ordered to migrate from Makkah to Madinah he said, "I need a guide." He is a prophet, why does he need a guide? To teach us, "I am a prophet, and yet I need a guide." For my external life, for my outer life, I need someone to show me the way to reach Madinah. For example, now we are showing my son how to go to Niagara Falls. We do not know, so we find an expert—by God's leave a good expert who will not give us wrong directions! So he is a prophet and he asked for a guide. Didn't he know?

Jesus ﷺ said, "One of you is going to betray me." It is true and this we believe as Muslims. He said "one of you"—did he not know who? He knew, but he did not reveal it. Prophets know, but they wish to show complete weakness and humility. Prophet Muhammad ﷺ also knew the way to go from Makkah to Madinah, but he teaches us to take a guide. They needed a guide to show them the way from Makkah to Madinah. And they reached Madinah safely with the help and guidance of that guide.

If we need a guide to cross a desert, what about for our spiritual life? It is more difficult. You certainly need a guide for that, and that is why, also, the Prophet ﷺ had a guide in the Archangel Gabriel ﷺ, giving him inspirations and revelation, and was guiding him into God's Presence on the Night of Ascension, that night when the Prophet ﷺ went to meet his Lord. So when he migrated from Makkah to Madinah, he needed an external guide; when he migrated to his Lord on the Night of Ascension, he needed an internal guide. It is impossible to migrate without a means. Without a means you cannot reach anywhere.

That is why everyone must find a guide to show him the way of truth and the way of reality. Without a guide, you will be in doubt whether what you are doing is right or wrong. With a guide, you depend on someone because he is an expert. As we said, the Prophet ﷺ took that guide to show him the way to Madinah. He did not say to that guide, "No, why are you taking me this way? Why not take me that way?", because he knew he was depending on his expertise.

The guide who shows you the way must be trustworthy. You cannot take a superficial or artificial guide and say, "This is my guide." If you take an imitation guide, he will take you to Satan's oceans of hallucinations and you will be lost. Many people follow such untrue "guides." At some point the followers will begin to have hallucinations, and they will think that they are seeing something. In reality they are experiencing hallucinations, and what they are seeing is non-existent. That is why a true guide is essential.

How do you know a guide? Once, Grandshaykh said, "To know that a guide is a true one, first you must see that he has completed his external outfit. If you see that he is incomplete in bearing the externals, it means that he has a defect in his heart. Do not follow him."

Anything in a Sufi shaykh—and we are speaking about Sufism, not about anything else—that is not the true external dress and manner of a true master, betrays a defect. Grandshaykh said:

> If you have a watch, and that watch is working internally one hundred percent, but it has no needles, it will not give you the time, so there is no benefit in it. Similarly, if a watch has two needles, but the internal mechanics are not working one hundred percent, it will not show you the correct time. So both the outward and the inward must be completely correct for someone to be a real guide.

We are not speaking about ourselves. We are following our master—he is a guide. He is our guide, and he is working one hundred percent, both outwardly and inwardly. As for us, we are trying to imitate him. That is why, when we want to look at a guide, to say, "This person is a true guide," you must see him complete the outfit without lacking anything. If there is anything missing, then you cannot follow him. It means that if he is missing something from his exterior, then he is lacking many things in his interior; for that is where people *cannot* see. When you know that people are looking at you, you dress well. But when people are not looking at you, you say, "Never mind, they are not seeing me." So you will have more items missing. If, in your outfit, which people are going to see, you are missing many items, it means that your "infit"—so to speak—which people are not seeing, is even more deficient. That is why such a person is not a true guide, but is disconnected. He might take you to a certain distance in the spiritual life, but he is cut off from any further levels. A true guide must have correctly completed his exterior, without missing a single item.

Grandshaykh said:

This is the first step in knowing whether someone is a true guide or a false guide. When you see this from him, then you say he has now passed, not the first test, but the first criterion. So we now consider his inner side.

How do you examine the inner side? First, you see if that person has respect for everyone, without the slightest discrimination towards any human being, without looking at their background—because they are servants of one Lord, the same Lord, and the Lord doesn't change. It is neither your business nor his business, because they are the servants of his Lord. He has to respect them, because they are God's creation, and have that light in them.

Then, after having respect for them, he must have love for them. Then he will want for them what he wants for himself and his children, to be and act also on their behalf, although they are not yet his followers but simply ordinary people. So he must show them respect and love.

Thirdly, he must show them humbleness, that is, he must be lower than them. He cannot say that he is higher than they. No one is high except God. If he will see himself higher than they are, then he is like Satan, who saw himself higher than Adam ﷺ.

These three criteria are the "inner accessories" of the true guide. For the outfit he must have the complete dress of a Sufi master. If your master is like that, then that one is a true guide. Follow him. At that time you can find satisfaction and all that you are missing. If you do not find someone like that, then look further. You will find because God is merciful. When you look, God will give. When you do not ask, God will not give. If you really ask from your heart, you are going to find. At that time, he will give you the key to your heart. If you are not really asking from your heart but only with the tongue, perhaps you might see one, perhaps not.

## Story of Ahmad al-Badawi

Sayyidina Ahmad al-Badawi ق, a very famous saint known in all Sufi teachings —may God bless his secret—did not accept a guide, and said, "I have no need for a guide; my guide is the Qur'an"—as the Wahhabis say today—"and the *Sunnah* (Way of Life) of the Prophet ﷺ," and he was trying to approach his Lord as the Prophet ﷺ said on his Lord's behalf:

> *My servant draws not near to Me with anything more loved by Me than the religious duties I have enjoined upon him, and My servant continues to draw near to Me with supererogatory works so that I shall love him. When I love him I am his hearing with which he hears, his seeing with which he sees, his hand with which he strikes and his foot with which he walks.*[68]

Ahmad al-Badawi ق was drawing near his Lord until he reached the door of the Divine Presence and said, "O my Lord, please open the door for me." He was not getting an answer. He

---

[68] Bukhari, Ahmad, #38 in an-Nawawi's *Forty*.

was trying more and more, until he met someone by chance. (We say "by chance" but it was not by chance, it was well-organized and pre-arranged—for it was God's Will to test him.) He saw that person on the street, an ordinary person, who looked at him and said, "O Ahmad!" He did not even call him, "Shaykh Ahmad" to give him due respect. He said, "O Ahmad! You need the key to God's Divine Presence? I have that key. If you want it, come to me and I'll give it to you."

Many people among us, because they are proud of themselves, refuse to accept facts and truth, although they know, as a matter of fact, that this is the right path. They are not accepting because their ego says "NO!" So Ahmad's ego said to him, "How are you going to accept something from him? Don't accept the key from him, accept it only from God." So he said, "O my brother, I don't take the key from you, nor anyone except the Key-Maker. Who are you? You are nothing."

Then he kept striving to reach the Divine Presence until he heard a voice saying to him, "O Ahmad, this life is the life of cause and effect. I will not give you the key. My Will is that the key to My door, for you, is with that person. Go and get it from him." Now the matter was settled. He had heard it from his Lord, and he accepted.

Now he had to find that guide. But that guide had disappeared. He had left him. For six months the guide was secretly observing Ahmad's heart, seeing him search for him to-and-fro, and pray to his Lord day and night, "O my Lord, send that person back to me." That person, finally, removed the veil—he had been there all the time—revealing himself, and Ahmad saw him at last.

(That is why there are many saints present here now. When our shaykh gives permission for a representative to speak, saints between East and West are opening their "aerials" or "antennae" to listen and receive from that association. There are many saints in spiritual attendance, because the only tap left open now of deep spiritual knowledge from the heart of Mahdi ﷺ, the Prophet ﷺ, and Jesus ﷺ—who is coming very soon—is the tap of Mawlana Shaykh Nazim ق. This is a truth that I know; not by hearing it, but by seeing it and feeling it: Mawlana showed me its reality. When he speaks in his lectures and gives advice, all saints are obliged to come and listen to him. And when anyone talks on behalf of Mawlana Shaykh Nazim ق and speaks with his permission, there are spiritual beings present, jinn, saints and angels, that come and attend with us. If people's vision is open, they can see this; if not, there will come a day when they can.)

So the guide removed the veil and appeared to Ahmad. Ahmad said, "O my shaykh! I found you." He did not find him, but the guide had removed the veil. Yet he thought he had found him. And he said, "O my shaykh, I accept you as a guide." He answered, "If you accept me as a guide now, you have to submit, surrender, give over your will to me completely. You cannot have a will beside my will. You have built your knowledge on a cliff. With a breath from the wind of the ego, it is going to collapse. I have to first build for you a firm foundation. So, look into my eyes." Ahmad looked into his eyes and that guide immediately removed all the knowledge that Ahmad al-Badawi ق had learned through books. "Through books" means that there are many things written that come from the authors' egoes. So he pulled out that knowledge out of Ahmad's heart and disappeared. He left him for another six months not knowing even how to say, *"Bismillahi 'r-Rahmani 'r-Rahim,"* and not knowing how to pronounce the holy name of God, Allah.

Everyone in the city now began mocking Ahmad al-Badawi ق, who had become insane after having been a great scholar. They thought that he was mentally ill because their understanding was limited. All they could see was that he was following someone who was making him crazy, but Ahmad al-Badawi ق knew that he had heard the voice of his Lord saying, "Your key is with that one." No one can make him crazy—he was only after that person with all his focus.

If Ahmad al-Badawi had accepted from the beginning, when that one came to him by God's Will, he would not have passed through this test at that time. Why make yourself pass through a test? When you find the truth, the correct guide, accept him immediately! Don't play games with your ego.

So the guide left him for another six months, then, appeared to him another time. In those six months, Ahmad al-Badawi ق had been searching for him again. When he finally appeared again, Ahmad said to him, "O my shaykh, I found you another time!" At that time, the guide looked into his eyes and through them transferred from his heart to Ahmad al-Badawi's ق heart, internal knowledge—the knowledge of the Book and its secrets—giving, giving, giving until light was coming from Ahmad al-Badawi's eyes, so much that anyone who looked into his eyes would die. After that he began to wear a veil (*burqa*). At that time he was able to enter into the Divine Presence, and he received that key he had been seeking so long.

It is impossible to reach the Divine Presence without a true guide that will open the door for you to show you where you are going. Ahmad al-Badawi ق was a great scholar who knew many things. He was proud of his knowledge and did not want to accept taking from someone else. Because of his pride, he wanted to take directly from the highest position. He was not seeing anyone higher than him except Allah. How, then, to take from another person? That means that there was no humbleness in his heart. At that time, he was missing one of the three steps necessary for God's servants. He had respect, he had love for human beings, but he was not keeping that humility in his heart to accept advice from someone else. And because he had left out that one step, he was unable to progress.

A saint, a master, must possess the three levels: respect, love, and humility. If you find one of them missing, then he is not a true guide. He will take you only a certain distance, just as we see with Ahmad al-Badawi ق who was able to draw nigh, to a certain extent, to reach the door of Divine Presence. He was unable, however, to open it, for he was in need of someone who had the key. He would not accept this need because he was proud of himself and his knowledge. He thought himself to be something. Later, he accepted. But he accepted then because he heard it from his Lord. That is why he had to pass a further, more difficult test. If he had accepted without self-pride, immediately that door would have opened for him, without the need for two years of testing.

### Humbleness in Approaching a Guide

When you find a guide and your heart is happy, don't listen to your ego. Say to your ego, "You are wrong! What am I going to lose if I accept that guide to be my master?" You will not lose anything. You are showing humbleness, and this is enough for God to raise you. If I come and say, "So-and-so is my shaykh," and take initiation from him, what is wrong with that? I am accepting; I am showing humbleness, so God raises me.

Showing humbleness is important. If you show humbleness, accept everyone, because everyone is going to be a guide for you. There is an idiom in our country, "They asked a well-mannered person, 'From where have you learned positive manners in society?' He says, 'From the one without manners. I observed what he did wrong, and avoided doing like him. So I corrected myself with the mistakes of others.'"

If you accept any person as your guide, even a wrongdoing person can be a guide. By observing him and seeing what he is doing wrong, you stop.

This comes from humility. Why then are you not accepting? Are you proud of yourself? Who are you? You are a creature from among six billion creatures in this world. Six billion human beings, and you are one. Why are you proud of yourself? We are nothing to God. There are six billion living ones other than you, not to mention those that passed away. And only one of you! So you are nothing! Why are you proud of yourself then? You do not have a political position, you are not in a spiritual position, so who are you to fight, and not to give respect, and not to love? On the contrary, you have to make friends.

Do not be a foolish and stubborn person by showing pride, anger, and disrespect to others. Out of these six billion, try to make ten, fifteen, twenty, forty friends—they will help you. To God, you are nothing; because you are one out of six billion, so it is as if you are nonexistent. It is like one over infinity. What will it be? Like zero. So you are zero. Why are you proud of yourself? Everyone is so proud of himself, you cannot talk to him! Why? Because ego is there, Satan is pushing you.

We have to try to have these three qualities: respect, love, and humility. When we correct our inner life and our external manners, then we will find the way to God. Since it is difficult to correct ourselves, we must follow someone that has already corrected himself, and take him as a guide.

This piece of advice from my shaykh is also important for me to listen to. I need this because my ego is so high. I am too happy with myself; I have to see myself as less than everyone, to respect everyone and to show humility. You have to teach yourself not to be proud. When you do this, you will win everything. So try as much as possible to bring down your pride and to increase your humbleness. Through pride you reach Satan. Through humbleness you reach your Lord.

# The Ocean of Knowledge in the Heart of Mahdi

If God is going to send faith to everyone in this life as he sent it to saints, everyone is going to leave his wife, or her husband, children, job, everything, and not do anything except bask in God's Love. That is why that power is not given to everyone but only to select people. My master has informed me and is informing everyone that we are of these select people, and that such faith is going to be given to our heart one day, and that day is not far off. Indeed, it is very soon. Every one of us that is connected to the Sufi teachings and Sufi masters of our Grandshaykh, Shaykh 'Abd Allah ad-Daghestani ق, and our shaykh, Shaykh Muhammad Nazim al-Haqqani ق, is going to receive that reward from Mahdi ﷺ—whether we reach to his time or not—as a grant from God to all of us, without discrimination.

## The Six Powers in Every Person's Heart

We now lack such faith; lack that light in our hearts. We are swimming in it a little bit, receiving the scent of it, leaving everything and coming here. How many miles has everyone come? For what? For that light which is *Haqiqutu 'l-jadhbah*, the certainty, truth, power and secret of attraction.

In each one of you there are six powers:

- ❖ The Power of Attraction of either objects or people to the shaykh—*Haqiqatu 'l-jadhbah*;
- ❖ The Power of Emanation or outpouring of experience from the Prophet ﷺ through the chain of transmission to the heart of the disciple—*Haqiqatu 'l-fayd*;

- The Power of Alignment of the shaykh's heart towards the disciple's, and of the disciple's towards his spiritual goal—*Haqiqatu 't-tawajjuh;*

- The Power of Connection to Divine power and favors through the Golden Chain—*Haqiqatu 't-tawassul;*

- The Power of Guidance to the destination embarked upon through the spiritual connection—*Haqiqatu 'l-irshad*

- The Power of Folding Time and Space—*Haqiqatu 't-tai.*[69]

These six powers exist in the heart of every one of us. If Mawlana Shaykh Nazim were to open that light in everyone of you, that light would attract all America—and America is still nothing. But that light is kept for the time of Mahdi ﷺ. There is no need for it now. It is enough to speak a little bit about it, but in the time of Mahdi unparalleled Divine grants, will be given, both physically and spiritually.[xxx]

Now is the time of trading, the belief in the Unseen. If Mawlana used this power through your hearts, then it is a "seen" power. Everyone would see and accept, and then there is no trade. Trade must be faith in the Unseen—*al-imanu bi 'l- ghayb.*[70] That is more powerful than faith in the Seen. That is why he is keeping that door closed, not opening it until the appropriate time arrives.

Today, he opened a very small ray from that attraction to the heart of our brother [a new disciple]. That caused him to be drawn here, and it is finished. He cannot be unsteady anymore but must run after that light, because he was feeling it in his heart and

---

[69] See Mawlana Shaykh Nazim's lecture "The Final Limit" in *Mercy Oceans' Lovestreams* p. 101-110.
[70] cf. Suratu 'l-Baqara, 2:3.

cannot turn away from it. That was a demonstration. If Mawlana were to open the power of that light for everyone, this world would not be enough. It will not be able to carry all of you. One of you would be enough to move this planet from its place.

There are powers that stand outside human nature, yet are made subject to mankind for whoever follows a perfect guide. If God Almighty opened what exists in the hearts of the special ones among the children of Adam ؏, human beings—what He is presently veiling from them—you would see wonders, things amazing not only for this planet, but for other worlds as well.

Sayyidina 'Ali ؓ was the only one permitted to use these powers. He was ordered by the Prophet ﷺ in every given period of time to project himself beyond the normal limits of our earth. If such a power had not existed in Sayyidina 'Ali ؓ, the earth could have been erased from existence, because of other-worldly, unseen beings, seeking to bring it under their control. [xxxi] God has said:

### *Surely have We honored human beings.*[71]

God did not honor those other creatures as He honored humankind. From their jealousy they therefore, wished to erase humanity from existence. That is why Sayyidina 'Ali ؓ was ordered to defeat these creatures by using the miraculous powers he was given so that they would not bring their tyranny to this earth. Were it not for him, we would have been in the power of other beings a long time ago.

Do not think our Creator is poor, having created human beings in one instant and then finished. He is originating creations every moment! He is the Owner of creation, Owner of that ocean that never stops, from the beginning whose "where" and "when"

---

[71] Suratu 'l-Isra, 17:70.

no one knows, to the end whose "where" and "when" no one knows. God is creating every second, every moment, every infinitesimal instant, and for every creation He creates there is a Judgment Day. Therefore every moment a Judgment Day is taking place somewhere and eternal life is being granted to some of God's servants.

What are we doing here now? We are playing. Sitting and making *dhikr* and chanting. If you want to go deeper inside, to see what God is giving to the heart of miraculous powers and miraculous knowledge, we find ourselves to be nothing more than dust. We are nothing.

You are select people and that light is present, along with those six powers, in each of your hearts. A time is coming when they will appear. That is why the Prophet ﷺ, with all the knowledge that he was taking from his Lord, reduces what I am saying now to nothing. What is in the heart now I cannot say—they would kill me once I step out of that door.

## Deadly Secret

Grandshaykh once said, "If I say what is in my heart, people will kill me. Now leave people: if I say what God and the Prophet ﷺ have put in my heart [he was one of the forty saints of the Golden Chain], saints will kill me." He did not say *people*, but *saints* "will kill me." There are 124,000 saints and, at their head, forty. The knowledge of the forty saints is different from the knowledge of the rest of the 124,000; it is higher. He said, "If I express what God has given of knowledge and honor to human beings, even some saints of the 124,000 cannot accept it. They will kill me." For that reason Abu Hurayrah ؓ said:

> *I have preserved from the Prophet ﷺ two vessels of knowledge. As for one, I have spread it to everyone; if I express the other they will cut my throat.*[72]

There are secrets in religion. Sufism teaches you how to be constructive, compassionate and helpful; how to love, how to be humble, how to have perfect manners, how to philosophize, and ultimeately, how to reach your Lord. Then there are secrets upon secrets upon further secrets, apt to make people go out of their minds. The tongue, the mind, and even the heart are powerless to grasp these truths. Moses ؑ asked to see his Lord:

> **He said: O my Lord! show Yourself to me and let me see You! Allah said: You cannot see Me, but look to the mountain.**[73]

Moses ؑ asked to see his Lord, that is, to obtain these truths that the mind, the tongue and even the heart, are powerless to seize. God answered that it cannot be, but told Moses ؑ to look to Mount Sinai. That is, to look at what was already around him on earth of knowledge and science. Mount Sinai here stands for all worldly science. "If you can look at the mountain," that is, "If you can penetrate the ocean of man's knowledge that comes under the name of 'Mountain,' you can enter My door."

Moses however, was not even able to carry the immediate knowledge that was already around him: and that knowledge, symbolized by the mountain, was reduced to dust! How then is it possible to enter that ocean of God's Knowledge? No one has entered the Ocean of Knowledge of Allah Almighty except the prophets and the saints.

---

[72] Bukhari.
[73] Suratu 'l-'Araf, 7:143.

Even Moses ﷺ, a prophet and messenger and one of the five great prophets, was unable in mind, tongue, and even heart, to grasp the knowledge given by God to mankind, the knowledge already present around him—what then of the knowledge surrounding God, the knowledge of Absolute Reality and Truth? And what about us, where do we stand in relation to Prophet Moses? We stand nowhere! We are nothing!

Leave alone the philosophers that write, the erudite, the shaykhs that claim knowledge, who call themselves People of the Way—where is Moses ﷺ; where is Jesus ﷺ; where is Noah ﷺ before God? Who can proclaim anything? No one. How then can we profess our knowledge, hold it up and say we are proud of ourselves? Who are we? As Abu Bakr as-Siddiq ؓ used to, we must say:

> O Veracious One (Siddiq), you are steeped in disobedience; dissolve in your Sublime Lord!

## Meaningless Titles and Degrees

Mahdi's spiritual power will appear some day, we hope soon. Everyone is proud of his knowledge, thinking himself to have achieved a rank and a title for himself. From whom is that title received? They are getting their titles from non-Muslim, non-religious, non-spiritual institutions and universities: Ph.D's in Islamic Studies; doctorates of Divine Law (*Shari'ah*). Relatively speaking, such titles are nonsense. They must get their titles from God; and no one can get a title from God; so it means no one knows anything. Those who get titles from God are only prophets and the veracious ones (*siddiqeen*). True people are rare. To find a true person living for Allah is very rare. We have a rule or formula in Islamic jurisprudence (*fiqh*), "If something is rare, it means it is non-existent."[74] This means it is very difficult to find.

---

[74] Arabic: an-nadir kal-m'adum.

And where are you going to find those people whom God mentioned in Qur'an:

> ***There is no fear nor sadness for the Friends of God?***[75]

In the mosques around America; in Canada; in Europe; in Arab countries? It is all over, finished. True people, as time goes by, are hiding more and more because so much tyranny has spread everywhere.

We pray God we shall meet someone that is a true person to take us to the ocean of safety. Until then we are like fish out of the sea, floundering on the shore. When we are in the ocean, that is, when you submit your will to God, at that time you are swimming in His will. Who is submitting his will to God's Will among those around us? No one.

We pray God will grant that light come to the hearts of people one day. And this day we believe, is very soon, as the Prophet ﷺ has indicated in all his Traditions, 1,400 years ago. It is imminent, because all the indications and signs have appeared. We are in the last days, the end times. And we ask our Lord always to see this in our lifetime.

The knowledge that the Prophet ﷺ obtained on the Night Journey and Ascension, which surpassed even the station of the Archangel Gabriel ؑ, is the knowledge that belongs only to hearts. It is impossible to express it with the tongue. In some people even the heart cannot deal with that knowledge. Philosophers write their opinions about the attainment of reality (*haqiqah*) in books. But they cannot describe reality because they do not even begin to know what it is. They speak about reality but you may ask them — what is reality?

---

[75] Surah Yunus, 10:62.

## Reality is not in Books

Show me one book where reality is described, or one philosopher or one shaykh who was or is able, to describe it. There is none. No one is able and there is no way to do so. It is something that cannot be spoken of and expressed with the tongue. The tongue is created; reality means the Reality of God. How can you express it with your tongue or in your writings? They can pronounce the word—*"haqiqah, haqiqah, haqiqah,"* and say "we are seeking reality," but this is only child's play to keep them on the right path.

This lecture comes from Mawlana Shaykh Nazim to show you the greatness of God and the greatness of what is around us, while we ourselves are small, so small. How can one describe reality (*haqiqah*)? Is the description of God something possible? Can you describe the Creator by means of something created? It is impossible. All such writings and books are nothing then; they are created things unable to describe the Creator. No matter how far humans push the limits of the description of God, they remain powerless to attain it and fall short of even beginning. All that you attempt to write is but a series of beginnings never reaching an end. It is impossible to reach any end because at every moment God creates, through His attribute Creator; and this is true unendingly, without interruption. So every moment there is always a fresh beginning of creation, and no end in sight to that beginning.

With all this, how can you pretend to attain absolute truth? It is impossible... Except when the day comes when you yourself end—your Judgment Day. When does your Judgment Day come? When you become nothing. When you are *something*, you cannot obtain one iota of that knowledge. When you are *nothing*, that is, when you have united yourself with the station of self-extinction (*fana*), and attained absolute unity with absolute reality, then your

Judgment Day has come. In such a way the drop of water that is added to the ocean disappears.

Abolish your identity and you will find His Presence (*huwiyyatuhu*). As long as you retain your identity, you are not going to approach His Absolute Reality. This advice is from the secrets which are in the heart of our Master and which he is receiving from the heart of Mahdi ﷺ. This is a mere whiff and still it is nothing. For what we have said is still on the tongue. What is in the heart is impossible to express.

In every one of you there is that ocean of knowledge that God has given to you because you are select ones. But to reach it, you have to destroy your identity—to be nothing. At that time, you know everything. How is this possible? God will show you how through your heart. But ask for it every night, before you sleep. Do not sleep—I am speaking to myself before I addess all of you—like animals. Do not sleep without thinking of your Lord, no. Sit before you sleep and come to your Lord repenting, dissolving, saying, "O my Lord, O God, You are the Absolute Reality, You are the Absolute Identity. Please forgive us, take away our identity, take away our will, and keep Your Will dominating us." At that time you will slowly find that ocean being opened to you. And when it is opened, it never stops.

This advice is enough for this whole universe. It comes from the heart of Mawlana Shaykh Nazim, from the heart of Mahdi ﷺ, and from the heart of the Prophet ﷺ. These jewels are not thrown into the hands of the ignorant. These jewels have been brought and put between the hands of those that deserve them, and you deserve them. Such lectures do not come every time—sometimes, and only for special people. These are very deep secrets of Sufi teachings, and you cannot find such things in books. When Mawlana Shaykh Nazim opens something, if that something is to be found in books, then it is not important. He only opens something that has never been written. You must know that every moment there is creation of knowledge.

They write things in books and then place references to Sayyidina Jalaluddin Rumi ق, Sayyidina Muhyiddin Ibn ʿArabi ق, Sayyidina Hasan al-Basri ق, Sayyidina Hallaj ق, Sayyidina Abdul-Qadir Jilani ق, Sayyidina Bayazid al-Bistami ق, and other saints. But this is not their time anymore. Their knowledge has become as nothing in the ocean of knowledge of the saints of this present-day Community (*Ummah*). Every second, there is creation of new knowledge. Previous knowledge is over and done with. It is now limited to its own time and place. Next to the knowledge that is in the heart of Mahdi ※, their knowledge is a mere drop in an ocean.

When Mahdi ※ appears, or gives the order to unveil this knowledge, people are going to dance with joy, because they did not, and will not, hear of such knowledge like that which will open up in his time. He will come on the Day of Reckoning at the end of time, when the role of this particular Community has ended, which will bring the end of all knowledge as far as this particular world is concerned. All the oceans of knowledge that had been til now forbidden to previous saints, and hidden within the hearts of later saints, will be unveiled in the time of Sahib az-Zaman (the Master of Time, al-Mahdi ※), to the point that the knowledge of all common people and all saints, with the sole exception of Mahdi ※ will become like the knowledge of children.

Imam al-Busayri ق wrote:

*Happy are you,*
*O gathering of mankind,*
*what ye have from Divine Support is,*
*a Pillar that will never crumble*[76]

---

[76] From Muhammad al-Busayri's famous poem, *al-Burda* (the Cloak).

and the Prophet ﷺ said:

*The best Community, the most favored Community, is the last Community.*

You must be happy that God has created you as the last ones in this cycle, because everything is going to open before you and within you. No one can see what you are going to see. And we cannot go further in details as there is no permission. God willing, this is enough—but Mawlana is giving something more.

When people make *dhikr* they are happy. They are passing time, whiling away time, like child's play. When God opens this knowledge into hearts, we will dissolve like salt or sugar in water. No one can carry that knowledge anymore, not even prophets. When God unveils that knowledge on Judgment Day, even prophets are going to dissolve. God has created us and honored us.

# From Love to Annihilation

*[A visitor asked, "Tell us about the station of self-extinction, maqam al-fana."]*

What shall I tell you and where shall I begin? The question you are asking is the stage that *awliya*, saints, need years and years of seclusion and practice to reach. How are we going to speak about *maqam al-fana*, the station of annihilation of the self, and how to reach it? If I tell you how to reach it, will you accept it and do it?

If you will do it, then it is very easy. You have to be nothing. You have to be zero. You must not exist. Are you able to do that? How to do this is a long road. It is not an easy way. You have to give everything up to God and to the Prophet ﷺ.

Sayyidina Abu Bakr as-Siddiq ؓ was trying to practice every positive manner and to leave all negative and destructive ones. There are five hundred orders which God has ordered us to do, and eight hundred prohibitions which God has forbidden us to do. You have to keep the five hundred and to leave the eight hundred. It is very difficult to reach that stage.

## Steps to Annihilation

The first step of that stage is:

- ❖ Love of God—*Mahabbatullah*
- ❖ Love of the Beloved—*Mahabbatu 'l-habib*
- ❖ Love of the Masters—*Mahabbatu 'l-mashayikh*.

The second level is:

- Presence of God—*Hudurullah*
- Presence of the Beloved—*Huduru' l-habib*
- Presence of the Masters—*Huduru 'l-mashayikh*.

The third level is:

- Annihilation in God—*Fana'un fillah*
- Annihilation in the Beloved—*Fana'un fi 'l-habib*
- Annihilation in the Masters—*Fana'un fi 'l-mashayikh*.

What you are asking about is the third level. You need to begin with the first level, which is the love of God, the love of the Prophet ﷺ, and the love of the masters. It means that you have to give up everything for the sake of your masters, for the sake of the Prophet ﷺ, for the sake of Allah. It means that you have to love everyone more than you love yourself. When you love your Lord, you have to love your Lord's creation. If you are able to love Him more than you love yourself, or love me more than you love yourself, you are on the first step and on the right way.

## The First Step is Love

Therefore try hard on this point: love people, all human beings. The first step on the stairs is love. To climb these levels is love. If you can, then—Begin! Say, "In the Name of God, the Merciful, the Compassionate—*Bismillahi 'r-Rahmani 'r-Rahim*," then go ahead.

What is love? Love means to give up everything for the sake of human beings. Do you want more details? You can know the details yourself. Everyone knows when he loves someone for the sake of Allah, for the sake of the Prophet ﷺ and for the sake of masters; at that time he or she will give all they possess. If you love a lady, and she asks you to bring her the skies, you are going to try to find a rocket to take you to the skies and try to bring the skies to her. If she tells you to bring her a diamond, you are going to try to buy her the best diamond possible. Is it not true?

If you love your Lord, it means you have to love every one of His creation and try to help them as much as possible. This will be the first step in response to your question. Leave the third level. To reach the third level, you must traverse the first level.

## Shaykh Nazim's Initiation

Before Mawlana Shaykh Nazim came to his Grandshaykh, he was studying chemical engineering in Turkey. There, he used to go to Bayazid mosque, a big mosque near the university in Istanbul, to see a shaykh with whom he used to sit and learn Arabic. That shaykh was a Sufi master of the Naqshbandi *tariqah*. Shaykh Nazim was attracted to him and knew that he was a saint. He requested *bay'ah*, initiation from the shaykh, but the shaykh kept telling him, "All right, tomorrow, tomorrow, tomorrow..." Time passed and he kept telling him "tomorrow." At the end of the three years, the shaykh said to him, "O my son, your trust is not with me. It is with my master who is in Damascus, and his name is Shaykh 'Abd Allah ad-Daghestani ق; go to him, and you will get your trust from him." Shaykh Nazim left everything and set out for Damascus in order to meet Grandshaykh. His intention was to continue all the way to the Prophet's ﷺ city of Madinah.

He reached Damascus, after a long journey and much travail, which we will not describe. At that time World War II was in full swing, around 1941. The French army was shelling Damascus. All the streets were empty, but he had the address of Grandshaykh's place. As soon as he reached the door and was poised to ring the bell, Grandshaykh opened the door and said to him, "O my son, come in, I have been waiting for you." He said, "My shaykh, I came to take initiation from you and then emigrate to Madinah and live there beside the Prophet ﷺ." The shaykh said, "O my son,

I'll give you initiation tomorrow, and will give you an answer on whether to go to Madinah or not."

The next day, Grandshaykh saw a vision. He said, "My son, the Prophet ﷺ is telling you that there is no need for you to go to Madinah. Your people are waiting all around world for you to go and teach them. In Madinah you are not going to accomplish anything. All of them there are believers, they are sitting and not doing anything. But outside people are in need of you. Now I will give you initiation."

Grandshaykh gave him initiation and ordered him to return to Cyprus, and then to Turkey.

It is a long story, but we take wisdom from it. When you take initiation—I am not telling you to do the same, Shaykh Nazim is a Grandshaykh, a master, and masters are different—look at what love will do. When someone is wanted by God to be a saint, then he will do something without a will. It comes out of him. What did he do? He went back to Cyprus. He came from a very rich family that had a large house in the best neighborhood in Cyprus. He sold that house and everything else that he had there, came back to Damascus and brought everything in front of his Grandshaykh. He said, "O my shaykh, I am coming to you now with this robe (*jubbah*) as my only possession in the world. I have nothing left."

Grandshaykh did not then say, "No, no, take it back." He wanted to continue checking his heart. He took it. Where it went no one knows. It disappeared. Later I found out where Mawlana sent this money, but for the time being, it was a secret and no one knew. Grandshaykh was not in need of money. What would he do with it? They are teaching people to run away from this materialistic life. But they take from people what they love, because everyone loves money. So they test you. At that time, he immediately gave all the secrets to Mawlana Shaykh Nazim. He trusted him with the secrets.

## Our First Big Test

These are tests. This is the first step in love. We knew Grandshaykh and Mawlana Shaykh Nazim always used to come and visit us in Beirut. I was studying medicine and my brother was studying engineering. Look at the tests. I am not saying this to talk about myself, but to give an example—I am obliged to say it. We also come from a good family of moderate fortune. One day we came to Mawlana Shaykh ʿAbd Allah and said, "O our shaykh, we are coming to you and do not want anything of this materialistic life to go back to. We want to sit besides you and stay forever."

Now look at the test and see how difficult a test can be. You are asking what is the Station of Annihilation (*maqam al-fana*)? That is not easy: you are asking about a level or position where you are non-existent; only God exists there.

We said we wanted to stay with him forever. He said, "All right, if you want to stay and do not want to go back..." He asked us how much money we had in our pockets and we put everything on the table. He took it, and we were happy that our Grandshaykh took the money. We were sitting and waiting for the next step.

He asked, "How did you come here?" We said, "By car." He asked for the keys of the car, "You are leaving everything; come on, give me the keys." He took the keys; there was no car anymore. He is checking the heart: any doubt in the heart (such as thoughts that the shaykh likes cars, or money...), and he will kick you out of his presence. He took the keys of the car and we were happy.

Then he said, "You are still wearing luxurious clothes. If you want to be dervishes and leave everything of this materialistic life, this kind of dress is not suitable. Take off your clothes and bring them here." We asked what to wear. He said, "Go to my center (he had a small teaching center, a *dergah*, nearby). There was an old man who passed away seven years ago, whose clothes are left in a basket. Take one set for you and one set for your brother." All the while he is looking at our heart to check us. We were coming from Beirut to Damascus, and Beirut was known everywhere at that time to be "the Switzerland of the Middle East," a very luxurious country. He was looking at the heart to see if there were any changes.

We quickly went to the mosque—we were happy!—took out the clothes of that old man, took off our clothes, and put on the old clothes. As soon as we put on these clothes, we were filled with lice everywhere. Our hair, our small beards, everything was full of lice. "Come!" He called us to his presence and was continuing to look at us—were we having a change of heart or not? Now if I say to anyone to do something like that, what is he going to do? He is going to run away! He will say, "I don't want this Path!"

This teaching is patience. This teaching is non-existence. If you love, that's it: you do everything. Then, he said "This is not enough. No *awrad* for you, no *wazifa* (devotions)—no need. You only have the right to carry the *miswak* (wooden toothstick), a *tasbih* (prayer beads), and nothing in your pockets. You have no right to take a shower except once every seven days. Go to Muhyiddin Ibn 'Arabi's mosque—where he is buried—sit there, display a small handkerchief and sit all day, carrying your *tasbih* in your hand and your *miswak* and saying "Allah-Allah-Allah..." People will pass by, see your handkerchief, and know that you are poor and collecting money. So they will come; one will put a dime, another a penny, another five cents... Collect that money, but don't take it: bring it to me in the evening."

He is looking at our hearts, again, to see if they are changing or not. It is not easy. This is because you have asked a big question and I am answering you. Here in America, people now say they are Sufis and they make *dhikr*, they give lectures, they give advice, they do everything. What do they know of Sufism? What do they know about non-existence? All of them are enjoying a high standard of living. Did they pass through such experiences? It is not easy. They cannot buy it! That is why God said:

**O believers, fear God and be with true people**[77]

because they have the experience, they will show you the way. This is the way: to be non-existent.

He said to us, "When you come home in the evening, don't come to me asking for food; we're not going to have food for you. But in that mosque, once a day, every day, they give out food for the poor, soup and bread. You will eat there. Then you finish collecting money and you bring it back to me. This is your work. And this is my way *tariqah*, for you."

Nowadays, people come saying, "We want to be in the Path." "All right, what do you want?" "We want to take initiation." They take initiation and they go—finished. And this is the Path. At least this is something and that is good. But where are the orders? They say, "Oh we are making *dhikr*; two thousand, three thousand, five thousand, ten thousand times..." You do *dhikr*, that is fine; but if you are given such a test, can you carry it? If you can carry it, then it is alright.

As Grandshaykh was talking, we were scratching away—we were full of lice. Now we are changing. They were biting and crawling all over us and there was not one spot where we were not scratching. We were not so happy anymore. We kissed his hand and we went to the mosque. He left us without trying to keep us. He was examining our hearts. It was half an hour's walk from his house to the mosque. No car, just dirty clothes and patches.

---

[77] Suratu 't-Tawbah, 9:119.

After fifteen minutes, we saw Grandshaykh's servant running behind us with the message to come back. We thought that there were more burdens coming, something more difficult. We went back. When we entered we saw that he had prepared for us our clothes and a hot bath. He said the test was enough for now. "You have passed this test." This meant there were many more to come. We took a hot bath and got dressed. He gave us the money and the car back and he said, "This is the Path—*Tariqah*; it is not something easy. The shaykh will test your love, to see whether you are going to obey or not."

## Lost and Found

One day in 1977, we came to Grandshaykh again. From Beirut to Damascus it is a two hour drive but there are Syrian checkpoints at the border. The checkpoint on the Syrian border can sometimes take a long time. We were coming one day. We reached Dahr al-Baidar, a high mountain pass which, they said, was blocked by snow and so we could not pass. We had to go all the way to Southern Lebanon, close to the southern border, and come all the way around in order to go to Damascus. We had left Beirut around three in the afternoon. We had to first return to Beirut, then drive south. We reached southern Lebanon around midnight. We took the wrong road and entered into an unsafe area by mistake. The people there would have killed us because that was a restricted area. Someone like an apparition came and asked us, "Where are you going?" We said, "To Damascus." He answered, "This is the wrong way! Go back." So we turned back and continued toward Damascus.

We reached around six in the morning. As soon as we came Mawlana Shaykh 'Abd Allah was there and said, "I saved you from certain death, because they would have killed you." We had entered a very dangerous zone at the southern border.

## A Test of Food

When we entered, we found Shaykh Nazim sitting there. Mawlana said, "You must be tired, so I am going to prepare food for you." Look at the test that is coming. We were sitting with Shaykh Nazim, telling him how Grandshaykh had sent us someone to warn us that we were in the wrong place, and how we could have been killed. Meanwhile Grandshaykh was ordering his servants to prepare food. Then food came. Grandshaykh had a small windy room outside his house, near the porch. He had no refrigerator, so he used to dry fresh meat in the sun and keep it there. He brought meat from that place. I don't know how they cooked it, but they brought the dish and put it down in front of us.

As soon as they brought the dish in, the smell of the meat in the room became unbearable. You could vomit from that smell. Mawlana Shaykh Nazim was sitting but making as if not to see or smell anything. It was a test for us. Grandshaykh was laughing, as if nothing was there. But you could literally feel the smell, as if something had died in the street outside days before. I was looking at my brother and he was looking at me. What to do? We were going to vomit! Grandshaykh put that dish in the middle and said, "*Bismillah*, eat!" We looked at that meat. You could see thousands of white worms, crawling inside, coming and going, in the meat! Maggots. They say 'nuggets' here, so maybe it is the same. All these white worms, nuggets, maggots, were crawling inside and out, and Grandshaykh said, "EAT!" What can you do? He was not eating, Mawlana Shaykh Nazim was looking—what could you do? We had to eat. If we didn't eat, Grandshaykh would throw us out. This was a test.

Our visitor asked a big question! This is the only answer he is getting! This is to show you what masters do when they want to give tests to followers.

My brother and I were looking at each other, trying to decide what to do. We noticed Mawlana Shaykh Nazim's eyes, they were telling us, "Do it." But how to eat alone? If they ate, perhaps it might be less difficult, but they were not eating, only looking. And we had to take and eat! First the smell, then the maggots... But there was no way out.

Either you eat or you leave. If you leave, it is finished. But when you have love in your heart for your shaykh, even if he tells you to eat poison, you will eat poison. Love makes everything possible. This is what is needed in the Path. When he [the visitor] asked me his question, I said that the first step is love: for Allah, for the Prophet ﷺ, for your master—finished. Love eats poison and makes it nothing.

## Love Devours Poison

One day, the Prophet ﷺ passed urine in a bottle. Out of love, his servant took that bottle and she drank all the urine. The Prophet knew, but asked her nevertheless, "What have you done with that bottle?" "O Messenger of God, I drank it." This is an authentic hadith which cannot be ignored. He then said:

> *Your stomach is safe from sickness and from fire forever*[78]

That lady never saw sickness in her life again. Love makes everything possible, including the impossible. Because that love that Allah put into our hearts is not from us, it is from Him.

We took a piece of smelly meat. The maggots were even crawling onto our hands. As soon as we said, *"Bismillahi 'r-Rahmani 'r-Rahim,"* and put it in our mouths, all the maggots disappeared, the smell changed and become good. Everything changed. That meat "melted" in our mouths, it was so tasty. It

---

[78] Al-Qastallani, Hakim, Daraqutni, Tabarani.

was a test. At that time only, Grandshaykh took another piece, and Shaykh Nazim took another piece.

Love makes everything. This is a road. The Naqshbandi order is a road full of secrets, full of knowledge and wisdom, but diamonds will never be given free. Diamonds have a price, and the price of diamonds is love. If you have love, they will give you your diamonds. If you don't have love, they will give you candies. Do you want candies?

There are plenty. Anyone who likes candies can take. That is why, when you go to Mawlana Shaykh Nazim, he is giving very beautiful words for everyone, and everyone begins to think himself a very important deputy of the shaykh, a big *khalifa* or representative. That is because Mawlana is giving candies. If he gives a test, who will stay? Very few. So, love brings diamonds. Unbelief or indifference bring nothing. This is the big difference.

## Walk on Nails

You want the secrets in this *tariqah*? You have to walk on nails first. Do you see the Indian gurus? They walk on nails. Walk on nails, and you will find safety. If you do not, and you want everything to be easy, you will receive candies. If you take the hard way, you receive diamonds. So choose which way you want.

Take the easy way at the beginning, we are not telling you to take the hard way. As you progress more and more, faith in your heart will grow and love will accumulate in your heart. At that time you will sacrifice yourself and say, "O my shaykh—now, whatever you want to do with me, you do." This is what we are preparing ourself to be—nothing in the existence of our shaykh. We are nothing in his presence and he is everything.

## The Anger of the Shaykh

What is the best manner that our shaykh likes from his disciple? What is the time that our shaykh is happiest with his disciple? Sometimes, when a shaykh has many followers—hundreds or thousands—and all of them are sitting, and the shaykh wants them to develop positive traits and to leave negative manners, he picks one out of the group and begins to shout at him, "You are bad, you have to get better, you have to be well-behaved among us..." All the shaykh's anger will focus on that one, and the shaykh is looking at the heart of that disciple. If that disciple does not show anger, the shaykh will be happy with him.

The shaykh wants someone to sacrifice him or herself for the benefit of all. He cannot say to everyone, "You have to be better; your behavior is harmful," because he cannot break their hearts. Everyone comes thinking himself to be the highest saint. In reality, each one needs a lot of polishing and work on his or her heart. So the shaykh will choose one that he knows to be advanced and begin to throw everything at him. If that one does not react in the opposite direction, the shaykh will be very happy with him. This is the best manner that the disciple can offer to his Shaykh.

When the shaykh likes one of the group, he always shouts at him because he can carry more. If the shaykh shouted at everyone they would all run away. They would not accept such treatment. But the shaykh knows that the heart of the one at whom he is shouting can carry that burden. The only one that Grandshaykh 'Abd Allah ad-Daghestani ق usually picked when he wanted to show his anger was Mawlana Shaykh Nazim ق, and Mawlana used to laugh. Even the eyes didn't change. When a person is angry, you can sometimes see it in his eyes. That was never the case with Mawlana Shaykh Nazim.

We have to make our hearts like mountains. Whenever the shaykh is saying something to break the heart, we must be serene. What is going to happen? We are going to progress; we will not lose anything. When the shaykh is angry with you and you are not showing anything, this will raise you. This is a good manner from the disciple to his shaykh.

Grandshaykh used to say:

The best one in the eyes of the shaykh is the one who, if the shaykh pours out all his anger—and the shaykh is never truly angry; he is angry at deeds, not at persons—yet to the disciple, it is as nothing. The disciple's heart never changes, he does not feel that he has been held for less by his shaykh. Perhaps all the others think that such a man deserves no respect on the part of the shaykh. In fact, he is the one most respected by the shaykh and the rest have no respect. He cannot shout at them because they would run away. The shaykh therefore gives them candies. They get only superficial respect.

He shouts at one to make the others listen to what their own mistakes are. An Arabic proverb describes a woman who wants to reprimand her daughter-in-law but is afraid to do so directly, so she shouts at her neighbor in order for the daughter-in-law to hear, "Hear, O my neighbor, so that you will hear, my daughter-in-law."

You cannot always shout directly at listeners to correct them. But you can shout at one of them, although he is innocent, so that others will hear and correct themselves. This is the wisdom we must understand when hearing Mawlana Shaykh shouting. It doesn't mean that he is angry. He is shouting at someone to make the others hear.

## EGO AND THE PULL OF GRAVITY

Every category of animal lives together. There is no mixing of different ones—all must be the same within each species. It is said that human beings are perfect, speaking animals. God has created us in perfection and honored us as He said in His Holy Book:

***We have honored human beings.*** [79]

Unfortunately, I am afraid to say that we are less than animals yet. Every category of animals can live with each other. We, either men or women, are also a category of creation—and yet no humans can live with each other without fighting. Do you see lions, elephants, or any other kind of animal perpetually fighting with each other? They do not fight though they are raised all together. Here, two of us will be fighting in the space of only one month.

There must be some secret there to make human beings fight with each other. Go to any center in the human community—churches, synagogues, mosques, Sufi centers—and you will see them fighting. Because there is something hidden in themselves, which is pride. Everyone wants to be "he-himself, she-herself" the one whose ideas, whose opinions, whose leadership must work, either in his house, his job, his group, or anywhere. Wives want to fight husbands and husbands want to fight wives, for the slightest mistake. At work, no one accepts someone else's opinion. In a group, one's opinion must be the first. This is never-ending. Why?

---

[79] Suratu 'l-Isra, 17:70.

Because God imposed over human beings their ego. When God puts that ego there, it will not accept anything. That is the meaning of the Qur'anic verse:

> *We did indeed offer the Trust to the Heavens and the Earth and the Mountains; but they refused to undertake it, being afraid thereof: but man undertook it;- He was indeed unjust and foolish;.*[80]

Because human beings want to possess everything. If you gave someone all of Montreal, he will not be happy and will look over to Ontario to see if he can have it. You can never make a human being satisfied with anything. If you give him gold, he wants diamonds. If you give him diamonds, he wants your neck.

## Nothing Fills the Eyes but Dust

Because man is so greedy, God made him so that nothing can satisfy his eyes except dust. Why? Because when he is passing away, even if you bring him all the treasures of this world, he does not want them. Finished—he just wants to go to the grave and be surrounded by dust. It does not mean that he does not feel anything. He feels everything. But when he sees how merciful God is with him, and how he was running away from his Lord, if at that time you give him the most beautiful lady or the greatest pleasures of this life, he will be running after his Lord because he is seeing the reality at the time that he is given "birth" into the next life, the Hereafter. That is why the Prophet ﷺ said:

> *Human beings are sleeping; nothing awakes them except death.*[81]

---

[80] Suratu 'l-Ahzab, 33:72.
[81] ʿIraqi, Al-Jarrahi.

If this is the case, why are we fighting? We are of the same family. Everyone loves his sons and his daughters. Aren't we all the children of Adam ﷺ and Eve? All of you in your hearts are now saying, "Yes, the shaykh is right." I can hear this. But as soon as you go out of this door, everything is forgotten. It might be that some men and women who came here will begin to fight even as they walk down the stairs—not even waiting to reach home.

## The Pull of Gravity

These elements from which God created humankind are trying to pull us back to their origin. What is their origin? Earth. Gravity is pulling you, because everything is ruled by earthly attraction. As a circle has an infinite number of radii that all emerge from its center point, so too do all human beings refer back to one point through gravity: the earth. Your spirit, which is coming from God's Ocean of Power through His attribute Al-Qadir, the Powerful, is pulling you up in the opposite direction, to your other origin—heaven.

In some games, they bring a big rope and tell one party to pull one way, and the other party to pull the other way, to see which side will win. Whichever side pulls more, the other side must be pulled across; no one may remain. One side must capture the other, not just winning, but bringing the others over. This is the conflict between spirituality and egoism—the physical part of man. Whichever side wins, pulls the other over. That is why you see all people losing. They are all falling towards gravity, towards this earth. Only saints raise themselves up, and they can raise their followers as well.

Now they are sending the space shuttle Columbia into outer space. There is no gravity there anymore. You can see them floating in the spaceship, without gravity. When Sayyidina Jalaluddun Rumi whirled with his group of dervishes, he used to rise from earth and levitate. There is nothing pulling him down.

His positive side overcame his negative side. His negative side cannot pull him down anymore. If we can make our positive side more powerful than our negative side, we are going to be beneficial people in the community. People are going to look at you and say, "This man's good qualities far exceed his negative ones, so we are going to try to follow him." However, if your negative traits outnumber your positive ones, at that time you are going to fall, and all those who are following you will fall with you.

## Pride: Chief of Negative Manners

We have to try our best to eliminate pride from our hearts because it is the chief disease of all harmful traits embedded in the negative aspect of the ego. If you are going to keep your pride high, then, of course you are not going to accept any advice; you are not going to listen to anyone; you are going to fight, and you are going to fall into bad manners. Our master's advice is to throw pride out of our hearts and to come to each other with love, not with anything else. God created us with His love. If He did not love us He would not have created us. Come back with love to each other, and bring this love to all those around you.

# SEEING THE SHAYKH IN THE DISCIPLE

Mawlana Shaykh Nazim can control you from wherever he likes, because he received custody of your spirit when you took initiation from him. What veils this from people is the ego. Since you have an ego, people look at you and still see bad manners. In reality, your shaykh is working on your heart now because you are in his care. This is the miraculous power, *karama*, of the shaykh. He doesn't care for the ego or for the physical body. His care is only for the heart, the spirit. He once said, "Nowadays, shaykhs give their disciples anesthesia as a doctor gives anesthesia to his patient before operating on him, so that he doesn't feel anything." So he gives us something not to feel that he is working on us, but he is working on our hearts. If you take away that ego, then one sees the shaykh in that person. Then it is finished—this is what is needed.

Why are you listening to me, accepting something that I say, while if someone else says something, you do not accept it? Because you see my shaykh in me. I am not giving myself credit, I am giving an explanation to clarify things. At some point, good manners outnumber bad manners. That is when the shaykh appears in a person. When you look at so-and-so, you may not be seeing the shaykh, but the shaykh is in him. The shaykh is there, but veiled by the ego and the negative traits of that person. He is not yet clean from his negative traits. The shaykh is preparing his heart.

The shaykh prepares your inner self. You have to prepare your outer self. The disciples that have the most "scent" of the shaykh on them are those trying hard to kill their ego and prepare their outer self to be good. At that time, the inner light that the shaykh is preparing appears more and more from them. That light is coming and you are attracted to them as you begin to "scent" the shaykh on them. Everyone that took initiation undergoes this heart operation by the shaykh. This is the explanation of the hadith of the Prophet:

> *My Companions are like the stars: any one of them that you take guidance from will guide you aright.*[82]

When we sail in a ship in the ocean, we look at the stars in order to find our way. They are like stars; you take anyone of them and follow, and you will reach.

The Prophet ﷺ said:

> *Follow my way and the way of my rightly-guided successors.*[83]

Why? Because he considers the way (*Sunnah*) of his successors (*khalifs*) as his own, although they might change some aspects or details. There is a possibility of change: and there is another secret there. It means that caliphs have permission to change; and what about the caliphs of hearts? They also have permission to change.

Anyone who is a successor (*khalifah*) to the Prophet ﷺ leads you to the truth. We have one shaykh who is the manifestation of these ahadith. He represents the secret of the Prophet ﷺ. When you follow such a shaykh, you reach the spiritual presence of the Prophet ﷺ. The Companions ؓ cleaned their outer appearance and the Prophet ﷺ cleaned their inner selves. The shaykh purifies your inner self and you purify your outer self. Anyone who has purified his outer appearance—finished: You will see the shaykh in him.

---

[82] Mishkat al-Masabih.
[83] Abu Dawud, At-Tirmidhi, Ibn Majah, Darimi.

The senior disciple being observed by the others may still possess some negative character traits. There is also pride on the part of the on-looking disciples, who are also trying to clean themselves. The senior disciple is in the same group, working hard with everyone, conducting prayers, reading, doing *dhikr* and other practices. But each person's individual ego veils the secret of the person he is trying to observe.

## The Shaykh's Representative

When the shaykh mentions someone it is one thing, and when you look by yourself and see the shaykh in someone it is something else. When the shaykh mentions someone, it means it is finished: there is no doubt, no illusion about that person's station. When you see your shaykh in someone, without the shaykh having mentioned that person, and see that the person can speak on the shaykh's behalf, there might be doubt about the position. But when the shaykh actually says, "That one can speak on my behalf," then it is finished. You have to accept. The shaykh knows if that person is good or not. You must not have any doubt.

What about that person whom the shaykh has authorized to speak on his behalf, and in whom he is appearing at the same time? It will be double the power. The shaykh had mentioned X, and told him, "Speak on my behalf." This is certain. At the same time, he is appearing in the same group in the person of Y, but concerning this you might be wrong, and you might be right. Now if the shaykh said to Z to speak on his behalf and at the same time is appearing in Z—if you follow Z, you can fly; if you don't follow him, this is from pride.

You are in the same group, and saying, "Why is that one better than us? We have to be better! We are the people of Montreal. Why should we listen to that one coming from Djibouti or Tunisia? No need." Or vice-versa, "Who is that one coming from Canada when we come from Arab countries?" All this is pride and nothing else. If you take away that pride, you will see the shaykh there.

There are some people who look at someone appointed by Mawlana and say, "He is like us. There is no difference. There is no need to listen to him. He knows a little bit more than us, but there is no need to call him, listen to him or seek his advice." This is also a big mistake, because they are thinking themselves to be something.

In Malaysia, Mawlana has appointed Raja Ashman to act on his behalf. When I go there, everyone leaves that appointed person—who happens also to be the sultan's son—with all the respect due to him, and they run to me. But I never accept. I go and sit and give respect to that one appointed there. He feels shy, then says, "No, Shaykh Hisham, you speak or make *dhikr*." But I cannot take his position there: he is the one responsible. You must keep respect. When Mawlana appoints someone in Europe—like Shaykh Hasan in Germany—I cannot go and tell Shaykh Hasan, "When I come here, I will be responsible, I am more advanced." No. I have to know my limit. But when I visit, Shaykh Hasan feels shy and pushes me forward. Despite this, I have to know my limit. I have to close my mouth, and not say anything. He will say, "No, you speak; you do."

## The Door of the Shaykh

This is what we have to learn. Once, Shaykh Nazim called me and my brother Shaykh 'Adnan, twenty or twenty-five years ago. He said, "Don't always go to Grandshaykh with all the questions that you have, asking for all sorts of clarifications. Don't go there, because he is an ocean of knowledge. If he gives an answer, that one answer from him is like an ocean in which you can sink and drown. You need to go through the door, and I am his door. Come, ask me; I will direct you. And I am saying this to you only once. Take it or leave it, it is up to you."

From that time on we did not ask anything from Mawlana Grandshaykh; only from Mawlana Shaykh Nazim. Either he would then go with us and ask Grandshaykh, or he would answer himself.

Nowadays, there are some "dogs" working for Mawlana Shaykh Nazim; "donkeys" that he uses as doors to himself. He is using them, so go to them, and only then go to Mawlana Shaykh. This is perfect manners (*adab*) and this is respect. You cannot enter the ocean directly; you will drown. [Asking a disciple] Why did Mawlana refer you to me when you asked him your question? He was able to give you the best answer. He is the ocean of answers! It does not mean that I have the answer to give you, no. It is to teach you good conduct, *adab*, and to teach us that you will be a witness for what he told you and for what he knew would be brought up in this association, and in order for you to be a witness on yourself that Mawlana referred you to us for your question.

You asked him something in London; why didn't Mawlana give you the answer? It was easy for him. Instead he said, "No, go and ask Hisham." Why? To teach us. Not for me to see myself, but to teach us respect and excellent manners—*adab*. He knew that this meeting would happen today, that you would mention this, and that we would all learn from hearing it.

If people don't learn, what can you do? It is up to them now. Anyone who wants to listen will receive support. It means, "Listen to him, whatever answer he gives you, I support him, and I support you, if you hear it willingly." If you had said, "No, my shaykh, I want the answer directly from you," then you would have failed in the test—but you did not fail. You said, "Yes—I obey with all my heart."

# The Saint of Rajab

If support accompanies someone, then that person is always successful. All of the ones present have that support. If not, you would never be found in such an association. Why? You might just go on as others do, happy with the materialistic life and its pleasures. But that light which is in your heart is driving you here. If there is no support, it will avail all of us nothing to wear red and black and turbans, day and night. The important thing is *Inayatullah*, support from God. Were it not to accompany us, we would never accomplish anything.

## The Month of God

Ahead of us begins a very important month in the Islamic calendar, the holy month of Rajab al-Haram. It stands alone out of the four months which God has declared sacred—Rajab, Dhu 'l-Qa'dah, Dhu 'l-Hijjah, and Muharram. It also opens the series of three holy months culminating in Ramadan: Rajab, Sha'ban, and Ramadan. During these three months everyone must prepare and keep himself, as much as possible, away from bad manners and sins. The Prophet ﷺ said:

> Rajab is the month of God, Sha'ban is my month, and Ramadan is the month of my Community.[84]

God gave you twelve months in the year, eleven of which are yours, and one of which belongs to God. What rewards God will give his slaves in His month, no one knows, not even the Prophet

---

[84] Ad-Daylami, as-Sahmi, as-Sakhawi, Jarrahi, as-Suyuti, Ibn Jahdam, al-'Iraqi, Ibn Hajar, Kattani, as-Sulami.

ﷺ. The work of prophets and angels stop in the month of Rajab. They are not allowed to know what rewards God is going to give His Community. It is in the hands of the Lord Almighty, Allah. In the second month, no one is allowed to know what rewards the Prophet ﷺ will give his Community in Sha'ban, except God and the Prophet ﷺ. What is accumulated of the rewards in Rajab and Sha'ban will be written for you and known to everyone in Ramadan: that is why it is the month of the Community. These three months are therefore very important months in the understanding of the Sufi orders.

In the month of Rajab, the Prophet ﷺ went through the Night Journey and Ascension, *laylat al-Isra' wa 'l-M'iraj*. One must keep himself, during that month, away from all kinds of bad manners and behavior. One of the most important days of the year is the first day of the month of God. All seclusions commence at the beginning of the month of Rajab. The most important seclusions that Sufi masters have performed in their lives always falls in that month. It is a holy month. If you do something more for Allah in that month, you are going to be rewarded with a reward known only to Him and to no one else. In that month, God's Oceans of Mercy, Love, and Rewards, are going to be opened for His Community and His servants.

Each year, all saints wait expectantly to see what rewards God is going to open to human beings in Rajab. All saints on this planet, from East to West and from North to South expect to see extraordinary things between Rajab and Ramadan. Each one of us must therefore behave well, especially in these three months.

Look at the mercy that God sends in the month of Rajab. If you did something wrong, don't run away; come to your Lord: He will forgive you. It is very important, because no one knows what God is going to give to His servants—not even the two angels appointed to write at the shoulders of human beings. Everything in that month is through God, and no one knows what God will put onto his or her plate, for the slightest good manner or act of worship done for Him.

In the time of the Prophet ﷺ, there lived a notorious highway robber. He went into the streets after midnight, and if he found someone walking alone at night in the street, he caught him, robbed him, sometimes beating him or killing him. No one was able to catch that person. The Prophet ﷺ used to curse that person in his time, saying, "That person is a wrongdoer, I will never pray on him and I will not bury him in the grave of Muslims."

That highwayman passed away after many years. He had a daughter and she could not find anyone to look after his body and burial. Because the Prophet ﷺ had reviled that person for his crimes, the children took his body through the streets of Madinah and threw him into a dry well. As soon as they they had thrown him into the well, God spoke to the Prophet Muhammad ﷺ and said:

> *Ya Habibi*, ya Muhammad! O my Beloved, O Muhammad ﷺ, today, one of my saints has passed away. You must go and wash him, clean him, cover him, pray over him, and bury him.

## One Can't Ask God "Why?"

The Prophet ﷺ was astonished, for all his life he had been condemning that person. Now that he had passed away, God revealed that he was a saint. How could he be a saint? But no one can interfere with God's Knowledge, not even the Prophet ﷺ. If God wants to make a thief a saint, no one can say "Why?" You must accept. That is why, according to Sufi teachings and the teachings of the Naqshbandi order, you have to look at everyone as being better than you. You don't know if God is going to raise that person's level higher than your own level—who knows? No one can know, therefore no one can interfere. Do not look down at people as if you are superior to them. You don't know whether that person, in God's Eyes, is a saint or not. Who knows? Always keep people at a higher level; show them respect and be humble towards them. Do not show ego and pride.

### Consider Your Self the Worst

God's mercy is so great that you are forbidden to look at people's outward actions, criticize their bad manners and call them crazy. Leave them; they have a Lord to judge them. Look at yourself; make yourself behave well, and do not interfere with anyone else. It is not your job to interfere with anyone. Your job is to interfere with yourself alone. Correct yourself, and leave everyone else to their Lord. Let them do what they want. This is the true understanding and teaching of Sufism: leave everyone to their Lord, and interfere only with yourself.

If you teach your ego not to interfere with anyone, then you are going to find yourself living in happiness. Then when you look at people, you will only see servants of the same Lord as yourself, and therefore, God will sometimes forgive them what they are doing. Do not say, "You are sinners: drinking, womanizing, doing this and doing that..." Leave everyone to his or her Lord. Teach people in general. Do not narrow down on someone and be specific.

God told Prophet Muhammad ﷺ, "O My Messenger , go, take him, and clean him." Immediately the Prophet ﷺ called Sayyidina Abu Bakr as-Siddiq ؓ and said, "O Abu Bakr, we have to go and pick up that person's body." Abu Bakr said, "O Messenger of God, you said that you didn't want to bury that person in a Muslim grave, for he is not Muslim!" The Prophet ﷺ said, "No! Leave ordinary Muslims. God informed me today that that person was a saint!"

What was that burglar doing in his life to become a saint? He was killing, robbing and stealing all his life. The Prophet ﷺ went into the well, took that person out with his own hands, and they carried him to his house with the Companions ﷺ. He cleaned him, washed him, wrapped him in a shroud, prayed over him, then took him from the Prophet's mosque to the graveyard known as "the Garden of Paradise," *Jannatu 'l-Baqi'*, a distance of fifteen minutes' walk. It took the Prophet ﷺ more than two hours to move from the mosque to the grave; all the Companions ﷺ were astonished at the way the Prophet ﷺ was walking. With his hands he had cleaned that man, washed him and prayed over him. Now that he was taking him to his grave, he was walking on tiptoes.

"O Messenger of God," they asked him, "why are you walking on tiptoes?" He said, "God has ordered all saints from East to West, and all angels in the seven heavens, and all spiritual beings to be present and walk after that saint, and there are so many of them filling the way that I cannot find a place to put my feet. Never in my life was I so surprised as today."

After they buried him, the Prophet ﷺ did not speak with anyone, but returned quickly to his house trembling and shivering. There he sat with Sayyidina Abu Bakr as-Siddiq ﷺ, asking himself what that saint had done, a robber all his life, to merit such a high degree of respect from God. Sayyidina Abu Bakr ﷺ said, "O Messenger of God, I feel ashamed to ask about what I saw today, it was so astonishing." The Prophet ﷺ answered, "O Abu Bakr, I am even more surprised than you, and I am waiting for Archangel Gabriel ﷺ to come and inform me of what has happened."

When Archangel Gabriel ﷺ came, the Prophet ﷺ said, "O Gabriel ﷺ, what is the matter?" He answered, "O Messenger of God, don't ask me. I am astonished also! Yet don't be astonished: God can do what no one can do. And He is telling you to ask that man's daughter what he did in his life."

## The Secret of the Highwayman

The Prophet ﷺ immediately went in person, with Sayyidina Abu Bakr as-Siddiq ﷺ, to the house of that highwayman.

Nowadays, ministers and secretaries of state—no, even a manager in a company treats everyone as if they were beggars at their door. They show neither respect nor humbleness.

The Prophet ﷺ, disregarding his own power and status as the perfect human being and the Beloved of God, humbly went to the saint's house to ask his daughter what her father had done during his life, "O my daughter, please tell me how your father lived." She said, "O Messenger of God, I am very ashamed before you; what am I going to tell you? He was a killer and a thief. I never saw him do anything good. He was robbing and stealing day and night, except for one month. When that month came, he would say, 'This is the month of God,' because he heard you say, 'Rajab is the month of God, Sha'ban is the month of the Prophet, and Ramadan is the month of the Community.' So he said, 'I do not care for the month of the Prophet ﷺ or the month of the Community, only for the month of my Lord. Therefore, I am going to sit in my room, close it, and perform seclusion during this month.'"

The Prophet ﷺ asked her, "What kind of seclusion did he do?" She told him, "O Messenger of God, one day, he was out in the street, looking for someone to rob, and he found an old man of seventy or eighty years of age. He beat him until he was unconscious and robbed him, and he found on him a small piece of folded paper. He opened it and found a prayer inside. He was very happy with that prayer. Every year, when the month of Rajab came, the month of God, my father used to sit and read that prayer day and night, weeping and reading, except when he wanted to eat or make ablution. After the month was over, he got up and would say, 'The month of God is finished, now for my pleasure,' and go back to robbing and stealing for eleven more months."

The invocation used by that man is a very important prayer which all are advised to read three times a day during the month of Rajab (see Appendix for this prayer). Mawlana Shaykh Nazim said that this prayer cleans you from all your sins and leaves you as pure as a newly born child. It is a very famous invocation in the Sufi orders. The Prophet ﷺ asked the man's daughter to bring him the paper. He then kissed it and rubbed this paper over his body. Do not leave that invocation, but practice it during the month of Rajab; keep reciting it, and God will give you, if He wills, according to your intention.

God told the Prophet ﷺ, "O my beloved Prophet, that person came and repented to Me in the most precious month of the year. For that reason, because he at least sacrificed one month of the year for Me, I have forgiven him all his mistakes and I have changed all his sins into rewards. Because he had so many sins, he now has countless rewards, and he became a big saint."

Because of one prayer, God made someone, who never worshipped all his life, into a saint. What about you, people of good manners, worshipping your Lord as should be done, coming to such associations to listen? You have a merciful God, a loving God: what do you think He will give you in return? Do you think that He is going to leave you?

## Count the Steps

For every step that you took to come to such a meeting, God will take away from you one sin and give you ten rewards. Whoever comes from two hours' drive, let them compute how many steps they came. Do not leave such associations, because you cannot get such rewards when you worship: your five prayers are an obligation upon you, but such associations are not an obligation. They are voluntary. If you come, you are therefore going to be rewarded with a very weighty reward. That is why these associations are very important. They will show you the shortest way to reach the Divine Presence. They will show you the shortest way to reach your reality.

With the simple practice of reading something which saints were reading, you can progress very quickly. Don't come to the Divine Presence riding a donkey. Come to the Divine Presence on a rocket: you will reach more quickly. Your ego is a donkey. Do not follow your ego. Leave it, for it will never take you anywhere except in slow motion. The spirit moves in very quick motion. Why? Because the spirit is something related to God. That light is coming from our Lord. Look at the speed of light: 300,000 kilometers per second. Do you think that your spirit travels slower or faster than the speed of light? Of course it is faster.

Now your mind is extremely fast: what then about your heart? Now they are trying to reach everywhere on earth quickly, using planes. What about the airplane of your heart? Its speed is such that whatever place you think about, you will find yourself there if you know how to use its spiritual power. Saints can be anywhere at any time and any moment they desire. They can be here, and the next second, they can be in China, Russia, on the moon or on the sun, or even in the first heaven, by using the power of the spirit. Do not underestimate what God has created in you and in every human being. No one can understand how that mechanism of the spirit works.

Why does one pass away the instant someone shoots a bullet through them? Who takes life's secret away? Why does someone pass away when they are fatally ill? The reason is the spirit is always trying to escape and break free from the cage of the body. When it finds a way it will escape and return to its origin. When you yourself, through the power you possess over your own ego, free your spirit, at that time you can control the power of the spirit and it cannot get away. At that time you can do miraculous powers through your spirit.

It was not long ago when you could find saints everywhere, using miraculous powers that no one can replicate today. There was one saint I personally knew, who could use his belt to call people living very far away, and he would do so in the presence of hundreds of people sitting around him. How does one send a message to someone who lives three or four hours away by car? That saint would simply pick up his belt, put it against his ear, and say, "Hello? Mr. so-and-so, please come over, we are waiting for you!" After three or four hours, that person would knock at the door and enter, telling everyone that he had received a call from the shaykh asking him to come over.

There are so many things saints can do because their ego is under their control. When the spirit controls the ego, you can do everything; when the ego controls the spirit, you cannot do anything. You have to always be a garbage container for human beings. Don't be afraid to carry their burdens. Carry and move. If you carry, God will give you more power. If you don't carry their burdens, you are never going to have that light in your heart. You have to be a carrier of burdens.

There was one saint who said to his Lord, "O my Lord! Make my body as big as your hell, and put me inside alone, and let everyone stay outside. I am sacrificing myself for the benefit of your innocent people. They are innocent because they have their egos weighing them down. If they didn't have ego, they would be like angels." Everyone of us has ego. It is that ego that is controlling you and making you behave badly.

All of you have to be examples for others, to attract people to our associations. This occurs merely by observing you and appreciating your good manners and behavior. When they are going to see you act badly, how are they going to come to these associations? They will never come. How does one acquire good manners? By leaving bad temper and anger. Don't show anger, whether in your house or outside your house. Don't pay attention if your wife is shouting at you. Let her shout: what can happen? Finally, she will get tired and stop. The same goes for the men— for whom we may use another expression than "shout" because they are men! You are going to bark and bark, and she will pay no attention, then you are going to be fed up and be quiet. But Satan never allows one to be angry except the other has to be angry: fighting follows. Therefore when one shouts, let the other not listen. And this must be applied outside in the community as well. Try to keep your anger down.

## Hold Anger

One day I was with Mawlana Shaykh Nazim in Madinah. At that time, Mawlana Shaykh used to take many pilgrims from Cyprus on Hajj wih him. He took them to a merchant to buy some prayer-beads. After they all bought beads, Mawlana Shaykh asked for one set of beads for himself. The merchant showed him some beads, and Mawlana Shaykh Nazim said to him, "Can you make a discount for me?" The merchant exploded. There is not a single foul name that he did not use against Mawlana. Mawlana did not even open his mouth. He kept his anger completely down. Afterwards, when we moved out to the street, we saw someone coming to the shaykh with identical beads in his hands. He gave them to the shaykh with the words, "This is a gift from me," and no one knew who he was nor where he came from; he disappeared as fast as he appeared.

When you keep your anger down, God is going to reward you. Do not try to take your rights by force. God said in Qur'an,

> **Whoever forgives and makes peace will take his reward from his Lord.**[85]

This is better than to take your rights by means of your hand—through the courts, for example.

---

[85] Suratu 'sh-Shura, 42:40.

Prepare yourself, in this month of Rajab, not to miss any prayers. If you are going to miss prayers during the day, try to make them up at night when you come home, before sleeping. Try to recite "Allah" in your heart 1,500 times a day. If you prefer to pronounce it by tongue, do so. Also recite one hundred times a day:

*Allahuma salli 'ala Muhammadin wa 'ala ali Muhammadin wa sallim.*
*O God, send blessings and peace upon Muhammad ﷺ and upon the family of Muhammad ﷺ*

God willing, this will give you power during this month and will prepare you for the following month of Sha'ban, which has other duties.

## What Saints are Expecting

All saints are expecting Mahdi ؏ and Jesus ؏ to appear during this month. Everyone must prepare themselves for tremendous events to take place in the world. Communism has already ended, and everyone is with America, and people are hopeful that there will be no more war in this world and that peace will reign everywhere. Suddenly, one crazy person may do something which will cause a huge world war to take place—Armageddon—something predicted in all holy books, the Torah and the Bible.

Directly after this predicted event, Mahdi ؏ will appear, and after him Jesus ؏ will be descend from heaven. Hajj in this past year was one of the biggest pilgrimages held in this century. Mahdi ؏ was present, as were all 124,000 saints and 124,000 prophets spiritually present at 'Arafat. Prepare yourselves, therefore, for the great event that is coming soon on this world. Do not think that this world will last much longer or that we have many years ahead of us. We are very close to the last days of this world and to the Judgment Day.

We do not busy ourselves looking at other people's worship in disapproval; rather we are the only group expecting Mahdi's and Jesus' arrival very soon. We are on the right track. We have met them. We have received initiation from them and accepted them both physically and spiritually through the power of my master. What I am telling you is according to true vision, not vague or imagined. Mahdi ؑ and Jesus ؑ are among you. Every association, either here in California, or in Chicago, or in Montreal, or in New York, or in New Mexico, is held under the name of our master who is connected directly to Mahdi ؑ and to Jesus Christ. Mahdi ؑ and Jesus ؑ must be spiritually present in all of these associations, at least to look at you and then go. Sometimes they sit, sometimes they only look and then leave, and sometimes they look from where they are.

These associations are the only associations in this world that are supported by Mahdi ؑ and by Jesus ؑ, not only in America, but everywhere they are held in under the names of our shaykh. All other places where people congregate—synagogues, churches, or other Sufi groups—cannot get such light as what you get in such associations. You see yourself as small in number because shining stars are few, but you are going to be like stars in dark nights for the human race.

That is what Mawlana Shaykh Nazim is preparing you for: to awaken people and call them to look forward to Mahdi ؑ and to Jesus ؑ. By God's leave, some of you will receive initiation from both of them in dreams. This needs some progress on your side in reciting the *wird* [prescribed devotions] given by Mawlana Shaykh Nazim without leaving out one night. After that, God willing, you will be meeting them spiritually, and we hope one day physically as well, and we ask our Lord that it be soon.

# SUBMISSION OF THE SAINTS

*[Talk following a quarrel and scuffle at a mosque in London.]*

**Obey God, obey the Prophet, and obey those in authority among you.**[86]

Success is only from God. We are very sorry that these things are happening, but these things must happen. If they do not happen, we do not learn anything. This has to happen and it was written so, in order to check the hearts, the belief and the faith of every one of us. No one can stop what happens. It is written, and who am I to object? This is not to say, "I am better... or, "I am worse... We must all take lessons from what is happening to others. The Prophet ﷺ never made mistakes, but sometimes, instead of praying four cyles (*rak'ats*) of prayer, he prayed only three.

God caused him to leave out one cycle, to teach the Companions ؇ to correct their own mistakes. This is why the angel Gabriel ؇ always came to the presence of the Prophet ﷺ: in order for the Companions ؇ to learn how to behave with the Prophet ﷺ, because the Prophet ﷺ cannot speak about himself.

## The Wrestler and the Shaykh

The following story has often been repeated by Grandshaykh and by Mawlana Shaykh Nazim, and I have retold it many times. It has to enter the heart. Only if you listen to it and keep it in your heart will it work. If you do not put it in your heart it will never work.

---

[86] Suratu 'n-Nisa, 4:59.

Someone came to Grandshaykh once and said, "O my shaykh, I want to take the Naqshbandi order from you." That person came to the shaykh wearing huge daggers and swords. He was from Daghestan, and you know that Daghestanis wear their moustaches big, pointing upwards. They are wrestlers, like some of our brothers here. That man came with all his ego, requesting the shaykh to make him a Naqshbandi follower. Grandshaykh said at first, "I shall never give you *tariqah*!" The man answered, "What! I am wearing a sword and several daggers, and I can punch anyone! I want *tariqah*! If you don't give me *tariqah*, I shall punch you!"

Grandshaykh looked at his heart: immediately the Prophet ﷺ informed him that that person had good intentions. The order came that, although he was a wrestler and wore daggers, he was to be taught to become a Naqshbandi follower. Grandshaykh said, "I cannot give you *tariqah* unless you listen to my order. However, before I give you my orders, I am sending you downtown."

### The Heart-crushing Test

One day, during the Lebanese crisis, in 1976, a big building full of goods belonging to my father was bombed and razed in downtown Beirut, and we were bankrupted in one night. We came to Mawlana Shaykh Nazim and he reacted as if nothing had happened. On the contrary, he was laughing. He said, "This was a test for you from the saints. They want to put you down in order to check your hearts."

We said it many times and we repeat it: shaykhs do not give you candies! Shaykhs squeeze you and crush you; then they look at your heart: if the heart is good, if the love towards the shaykh is not changing, then they give you your secrets. If that love is changing, then what is the benefit?

A follower of Sayyidina 'Abdul-Qadir Jilani ق passed away one day, and the angels came to him in the grave to question him:

Who is your Lord?

'Abdul-Qadir Jilani.

Who is your prophet?

'Abdul-Qadir Jilani.

What is your book?

'Abdul-Qadir Jilani.

What is your religion?

'Abdul-Qadir Jilani.

These angels were innocent: they had to take him to hell because he kept giving the wrong answers! What is this "'Abdul-Qadir Jilani?" They started taking him away. Immediately 'Abdul-Qadir Jilani ق appeared and said, "Why are you taking him to hell? He said my name: therefore, ask me the questions. If you were to cut that follower of mine into small pieces and then put him into a grinder, he would still say, "Abdul-Qadir Jilani.' His love will never change. You can throw him into hell, he will never feel it: I will feel it, not him. He has vanished in me. His existence is with my existence and he cannot feel except through me."

At one time or another, Mawlana sends tests to everyone of us and looks into hearts, searching to see whether love is changing or not changing. Is faith changing or not changing? Does he destroy a building and goods worth more than ten million dollars? He does not care; he cares only for steadfast hearts. This is what the shaykhs want. They are not seeking the pleasures of a materialistic life.

Grandshaykh ordered that wrestler to go downtown to the market and to look for a person carrying lamb intestines on his back, "Go behind him and slap him on the neck with the flat of your hand. See what he says and report to me." The wrestler—because he was a wrestler—was very happy to have to run such an errand. If this was the Naqshbandi order, *Alhamdulillah*, praise God, then I will slap and punch my way to my secret! "Of course, O my shaykh! This is my job, to slap people! I will gladly go and slap him, not once, but hundreds of times!" "No," said Grandshaykh, "only once!"

The wrestler went downtown and looked for that person. He found him, came up to him from the back, raised his hand, and slapped him on the neck with all his strength. That person looked back at him with anger in his eyes—but said nothing, and continued on his way. The wrestler was angry, because he expected another reaction: he expected a bad reaction, so that he could beat him two or three or four times, or knock him out with a good punch. But now he had to come back to the shaykh and report. "O my shaykh, I saw something very extraordinary today. When I beat him, he did not react, but he looked at me in anger, and I waited for him to come at me in order to finish him off, but he never did!" Grandshaykh said, "Never mind."

The next day, Grandshaykh told him, "Go now to the same place downtown. You will find another person selling lamb stomachs." At that time, they used to hang all those parts at the meat market and sell them. "With this one you may use more force and roughness when you beat him. Then see what he says and come back and tell me." "O my shaykh," the man answered, "your order is my desire! I will beat everyone for you! This is a very easy order." He went downtown, found the person that the shaykh told him to look for, and with all his power, knocked him down with a big punch. The man fell down with all the meat that he was carrying. As he was lying down, he turned around and smiled at the wrestler without saying anything. Then he picked up everything and left. The wrestler was even angrier than the first time. Why was that person not reacting in order for him to take his dagger and finish him off? He came back to his shaykh and told him what he had seen.

The next day, Grandshaykh said, "I am sending you to a farm and you are going to see a very old man plowing the field. Now don't use your hand, because this is an old man. He needs something better: you have to use a stick on him!" Now the wrestler began to think: Why did the shaykh say to slap and punch the young people? Was it not better for me to use the stick against them, rather than that old person? But the shaykh went on and said, "Use the stick with all your power, and let it break on his back! Don't come back to me if the stick does not break on his back."

Look at the secrets of the Naqshbandi way: When Moses ﷺ came, he said:

### *an eye for an eye and a tooth for a tooth*[87]

meaning that if someone strikes you, you have to strike him back. In that principle there is an emphasis on physical power and control—as is right according to that time, yet they are still using it now. When Jesus ﷺ came, he said, "If someone slaps you on your right cheek, give him your left." This means that there is still will there: as if you are saying, "Fine, beat me on this side too." You are still demonstrating control, self-will. In the Naqshbandi order, you do not have permission for even that.

Now, something is coming into the heart of that wrestler and changing his heart. But he did not reject the order of the shaykh. Now, if the shaykh tells you to beat someone with a stick, what are going to say? You will reject that order. The disciple took the stick and went, but he was afraid now. Why must he beat that old person? Nevertheless he went to the field and found him, as the shaykh had said, plowing the field. He came up behind him, and remembered that the shaykh ordered him to break the stick on the old man's back. He was happy and sad at the same time; though in the first two incidents he had been thoroughly happy!

---

[87] Suratu 'l-Ma'ida, 5:44-45.

He took the stick and brought it down on the old man's back. But because the wrestler had mixed feelings, he did not hit him with sufficient strength to break the stick. As soon as he struck the farmer, the farmer struck the plow with his foot in order to plow more quickly, without looking behind him. The wrestler thought, "I must break the stick." With all his power now, he struck him again, still not breaking the stick. The farmer, in his turn, struck down the plow with all his power and the cow was going more quickly, so much so that the farmer was dragged on his knees. But the wrestler had to break the stick, so he raised the stick for the third time and, with all the power that he could summon, he slammed it on top of the old man's back and broke the stick.

The poor old man fell down, but immediately he got up on his knees and came crawling to the wrestler. Without a word, he seized his hand with the words, "Please, give me your hand and let me kiss it. Because of my sins, my shaykh has sent you to me in order to correct me. I know I am making mistakes and you were an instrument for my correction." The old man said this although he was in not need to be corrected, because he was already a "corrected" person: He was a disciple in the Naqshbandi order, which means that he had attained a high degree. He continued, "I caused your hand to feel pain by having to beat me harder. Please forgive me, and do not speak against me in the Judgment Day, in the presence of God, in the presence of the Prophet ﷺ and in the presence of my shaykh! I am ashamed before my shaykh, who sent you to me to correct me. Please forgive me for causing pain to your hand." He did not even mention his own back.

It was as if he had thrown cold water on that wrestler. He was melting. He went back to Grandshaykh feeling greatly ashamed. Once there, Grandshaykh told him to sit and explained everything to him. "O my son, the first one that you met was at the first level, a Beginner who has not yet entered the Naqshbandi order. When you slapped him, he only looked at you, but he looked in anger. It means that he knows this is from me and that I am sending you to correct him, but he still has anger in his heart, and that is why you can see it on his face. The second one is at the second level, a *musta'idd*, 'ready' to enter and become a disciple in the Naqshbandi order. When you hit him, he looked at you, but he was laughing, and this shows that there is a will, as if he were saying, 'O my shaykh, I know that this is from you and I am laughing. You are testing me, and I am going to resist.' Therefore there is still a will there."

## Don't Consider Anything Insignificant

Look at the small things that the shaykh observes. Mawlana says something: people resist; object; reject. If you reject, why then are you following Mawlana? Are you not following to learn? Learn, therefore, as much as possible. Do not reject, do not resist, do not object. Whatever Mawlana wants to put you in, whether boots, or shoes, or bare feet, do not say, "Why?" Accept. What is it going to be? Do you want the love of the master or the love of the people? Do you want to get the title of "Shaykh" from God and from heaven, and from your shaykh, or do you want that title to come from people who say that you are a shaykh?

The third man whom the wrestler had to beat, when he fell down and the stick was shattered on his back, turned around and kissed the hand of his aggressor. He said to him, "Please forgive me for having caused pain to your hand because of my sins: for if I were not a sinner, my shaykh would have never sent you to me to correct me." That person had no sins: he was in the Naqshbandi order and he was eighty years old. Yet he considered himself a sinner and accepted to consider himself so. He does not want to tell his ego that he is something. You must always put your ego down and say to your ego, "Even though you are the biggest saint, you are nothing." As Mawlana Shaykh Nazim says, "I am always trying to tell my ego that I am dust—non-existing." You cannot give anything to your ego to be proud of. Otherwise, it will kill you. Rather, you have to kill your ego.

That old man said, "Please forgive me for hurting your hand. In the Judgment Day, don't come before God and ask revenge from me. Therefore, let me kiss your hand."

## Always Consider Yourself in the Wrong

It is very important for someone who is not mistaken, to consider himself mistaken. This is the biggest sacrifice. When Sayyidina Bayazid al-Bistami ق went on a ship during a storm, the captain thought that the ship was going to capsize and shouted, "There must be a sinner among us! We have to throw that sinner into the sea in order for it to calm down." Sayyidina Bayazid looked at them and thought, "These are stupid people; they are going to throw some innocent into the sea." He sacrificed himself and said, "I am the sinner." They threw him into the sea, and the sea calmed down.

To consider yourself a sinner although you are not one—this is the biggest sacrifice. "That old person of eighty years," Grandshaykh went on to say, "is a disciple (*murid*) in the Naqshbandi order, because he sees everything as coming from his shaykh; not from X, Y or Z." Mawlana Shaykh is bringing us to this place [Peckham Mosque in London] every year in order to test us, because this is the place for experiment and experience. In the streets of ordinary life there is no place for experiment. Here, there are difficulties. It is like pilgrimage: everyone fights the other, because it is too crowded and there are too many problems. You have to learn patience.

## Everything Comes from the Shaykh

You must see everything here, most especially inside this mosque, as coming from the shaykh. Even if people around us seem to be suffering, men as well as ladies, we must know in this mosque that we are in a place of experiments and that we are receiving wisdom. The shaykh is looking at everything. Anyone that misbehaves must be left to their shaykh. Your shaykh will take your revenge or chastise the offender. Don't take your rights by means of your hand. If you take it by your hand, he is going to send another person to take his retribution from you also. Leave everything to the shaykh. Don't say, "The shaykh doesn't know this is going on." The shaykh knows, but will interfere only when it is needed.

Let us understand the wisdom of coming here from all parts of the world. There are many mosques and places of worship in your respective countries. Why are you coming here? You are coming here for the sake of Mawlana Shaykh Nazim. You must behave, therefore, in the way that he would like you to. We must not, therefore, act against his will. We must act according to his teachings. Let everyone look at the other as being motivated and moved by the will of the shaykh: then there will be no fighting, and no overcrowding. But if some people want to eat the best food and reach it first, of course people will be getting angry on behalf of their ego.

Mawlana Shaykh Nazim brings you here and lets you face this ego: it is better than putting you in seclusion. This type of seclusion is better for you than a forty-day seclusion that will drive everyone away. That is the hardest seclusion. When he orders you to enter a forty-day seclusion, you will not be able to carry it. Your ego is going to come and kill you. No one has this much experience yet. And if you do not have this experience, you have to kiss the feet of Mawlana Shaykh to thank him for not putting you into such a seclusion. The experience in the mosque is enough for you, because it teaches patience and gives you training.

## The Final Lesson

Then Grandshaykh said to the wrestler, "O my son, this is not enough; I am going to take you for a picnic, come with me." Now comes the most important wisdom. That wrestler who had come by way of punching and beating everyone, at the end of the three days he had become an ant whom everyone could trample underfoot and crush. His pride and ego came down because of what Grandshaykh had shown him. They went to an apple orchard full of apple-trees. "O my son," he said, "Look at that tree full of apples. Now take that big stone and throw it against the tree and see how it will react."

The wrestler understood this example. Throwing the stone represented his physical power, and his urge to assault everyone.

## Don't Discriminate Between God's Servants

This is a lesson for everyone present. We are all at the same level. Even a child in this mosque is at the same level with the adults. Ladies and men are at the same level: there is no discrimination in Mawlana Shaykh Nazim's book. God does not like discrimination. Do not say "white, black, yellow, green, British, Canadian, German, American, Arab..." There is no such thing. If you say there are such things, then Mawlana is Cypriot, so let no one follow him but Cypriots. But you cannot say this. Why then this discrimination among nations? Remove it from your hearts. The Prophet ﷺ said:

> *There is no difference between Arab and non-Arab except in righteousness.*[88]

This is despite the fact that the Prophet ﷺ himself was an Arab. Consider that it is the same with followers of Mawlana Shaykh: there is no difference between them except through righteousness.

The wrestler took the stone and hurled it against the apple-tree. The blow was so powerful that one of the apple-tree's

---

[88] Bayhaqi, Tirmidhi's *Sunan*, Ahmad's *Musnad*.

branches broke and ten apples fell down. The shaykh said, "My son, what have you done to that tree? You have harmed that tree by throwing that stone at it and breaking that branch. You broke, you harmed, you hurt! You punched and you killed! But what did that tree do to you in return? It sent you ten apples in return, each one sweeter than the other."

The wrestler understood the meaning behind this example. The tree's utter acceptance of the breaking of its branches and dispensing its fruits for all to eat from, represented those who leave their will for their shaykh's.

This means that if anyone harms you, you should return his harm with good. If someone hurt you, you must say, "O my Lord, O my Prophet, O my shaykh! That person hurt and harmed me; because he harmed me, you are going to give me rewards. That reward, I am giving back to him, and I am sacrificing that reward to him in order that he will be better. I am giving everything to him." This is what the Prophet ﷺ said we must do when he said:

> *None of you is a believer until he loves for his brother what he loves for himself,*[89]

and the teachings of the Naqshbandi order "love for your brother more than what you love for yourself." When someone hurts you, you have to repay it with a reward.

Mawlana said that God has made a promise to the saints of the Naqshbandi order that in the Judgment Day, He is going to call all the followers of saints. First He is going to ask all the devout servants, "Did you follow anyone to the door of the Prophet?" If they say, "Yes, I followed such-and-such shaykh," God is going to call that shaykh and tell him, "This is your disciple, I am sending him to Paradise with you." But if the answer is, "O my Lord, I did

---

[89] Bukhari and Muslim.

not follow any saint," God will then ask, "Did you hear the name of any saint?" If they answer, "Yes, I heard of a saint called Shaykh Nazim," or "I heard of a saint called Shaykh ʿAbd Allah," or "Shah Naqshband," God will call that saint and say, "That person heard your name: take him, I am sending him to Paradise with you."

Mawlana said that if someone says, "O my Lord, I heard about that saint, but I did not like him and I cursed him," God is going nevertheless to call that saint and say, "That person cursed you, but take his sins and carry his burden; it is enough for anyone to hear about your name for Me to send him to Paradise." God has given this gift to saints. Even if you say about Mawlana Shaykh, "He is bad," it is enough cause for Mawlana to take you to Paradise with him.

These are secrets of the Naqshbandi order. That is the reason Mawlana Shaykh does not care about people who insult him, criticize or defame him—especially from our groups—through their bad behavior. If anyone in the street hears about Mawlana Shaykh but does not feel love for him, it is enough for Mawlana to take him, for that secret Mawlana is spreading through East and West. Mawlana is under the spiritual order of the Prophet ﷺ to travel East and West, and no single saint has travelled as much as Mawlana has travelled. Saints used to stay in their places and people would come to them. Now, because we have reached the last days of this world, Mawlana Shaykh is spreading this secret through East and West. If anyone can hear his name, it is enough to be counted among his group.

Keep this love in your heart. As Mawlana Shaykh keeps everyone in his heart, even the ones cursing him, you also have to carry someone's offence if they hurt you and harm you, and you have to give them goodness and rewards in return. Remember this especially among the people of our group. Mawlana Shaykh uses you as tests to check everyone's hearts. If people under the test did not "misbehave" openly as they do, none of the other people would learn anything. The mistake would still be there. Open incidents can only be judged by Mawlana, however, and at the same time they serve as lessons to everyone. We have no right to interfere. We have to take this as example and learn how to behave from now on.

Grandshaykh showed the wrestler who came to him with daggers and swords how to be humble and leave his ego. If someone hurts him, he now had to give goodness in return. We have to learn the same thing. If we are to follow our shaykh's way, you have to accept not to return a hurt to someone who injures you; rather reward him. This is very important. Let us put it into our minds and our hearts.

## Repay Harm with Mercy

The Prophet ﷺ said, when he was stoned by unbelievers, raised his head and prayed:

*O my Lord, reward my people for they are ignorant.*[90]

This is a long way from Moses' ﷺ injunction and even Jesus' ﷺ. The Prophet ﷺ said, if anyone harms or hurts you, ask forgiveness for him from God, and God said in Qur'an:

**Whoever forgives and makes peace will take his reward from his Lord.**[91]

---

[90] Zubaydi and as-Suyuti.
[91] Suratu 'sh-Shura, 42:40.

# The Naqshbandi Golden Chain

The head of every lecture is:

> *Obey God, obey the Prophet, and obey those in authority among you.*[92]

By obeying God you are obeying the Prophet ﷺ, and by obeying the Prophet ﷺ you are obeying God. Therefore, always keep your Lord and the Prophet ﷺ in your heart; and when you obey your teacher, it means you are obeying the Prophet ﷺ.

A teacher is very important. Everyone must have a teacher. Without a teacher, no one can progress and no one can find his way and his path. Even the Prophet ﷺ, and all messengers that God has sent to this world, had teachers. They had the archangel Gabriel ؏ as a teacher. That is why we have to take a teacher that will show us the way to the Prophet ﷺ and to God. Do not think you can arrive anywhere without one; it is impossible. By yourself you can never arrive anywhere because if you lose the way, you will be truly lost. So use someone who knows the way, who has travelled that path before and is experienced. He will take you by the hand and lead you directly to your goal without wandering here or there and getting lost.

## The Unbroken Lineage

That is why we have a Golden Chain. That chain of teachers and masters, all related to each other, goes back without interruption to the Prophet ﷺ. This is what we need: a direct chain. We don't want a chain that is broken somewhere. A pipe

---

[92] Suratu 'n-Nisa, 4:59.

carrying water underground from one village to another has to be completely whole. If there is one hole somewhere, the water will never arrive. If that chain of saints is broken you can never arrive to the Prophet ﷺ.

In every belief or faith, one has to be connected to the origin. That is why you have to know your teacher. Some people, if you ask them, "Who is your teacher?" will answer, "so-and-so." And who is so-and-so's teacher?

Now, we are not against any kind of belief, for all beliefs will take you to your destination; but understand what we are asking: who is your teacher's teacher? Many will not know what to answer. Some might say, "His origin comes from 2,000 years or 3,000 years or 6,000 years of mystic teaching and saints." Then what is the condition of that "pipe" of several thousand years' length? Who are the teachers that form it, the masters and grandmasters that transmitted it? No one knows; they know two, three or four teachers; then that knowledge stops.

A tree without roots doesn't give fruit. A tree that is only lightly-rooted in the ground will be thrown down by the first wind. Its grounding is too weak. A teacher must never be "grafted on"; for in that case one will not know who his teacher, his grandteacher, his great-grandteacher, and so on are, back to the origin of your path. That is why Sufi teachers are the most connected and most powerful masters in the world: they have true connection, they know their origin. If you don't know your origin, you are either not connected anywhere, or you don't know where you are connected.

From your teacher until the present, can anyone give us a count of their chain of teachers? Give us a sequence of teachers, do not simply mention a name from 3,000 years ago. We want an uninterrupted chain, without a single one missing. Often you cannot find such a chain. In mysticism we can find many such chains, particularly in the Sufi tradition. Through such chains we can reach the original message, without interruption, for it comes directly from one master to another.. That is why you need a connected spiritual teacher to take you to your destination.

Here is knowledge taken from the heart of the Prophet ﷺ and handed down through that chain of teachers. You cannot find it in any book.

## The Water of Life

Our Grandshaykh, God bless his secret, said that as soon as he was born, the Prophet ﷺ was taken by angels from his mother. As they took him, they were present, in the blink of an eye, in the Ocean of The Ever-living, Al-Hayy. God has ninety-nine Divine Attributes, and each one is a vast ocean of knowledge which no one can comprehend. One of those oceans is that of Al-Hayy, the Alive, the Ever-living. Whoever knows the secret of that Divine Name never dies. He lives always—not by himself, but with everyone, because everyone lives by means of the light of God in his heart. When you are swimming in the attribute of that holy Name of God, it means that you possess that light; that you are in every person and know what every person is doing.

That is where the Prophet ﷺ was taken by the angels, who were ordered to bathe his heart in *Mau 'l-hayat*—the Water of Life. As soon as they placed his heart in the Water of Life, he immediately possessed and was possessed by, and dressed with, *An-Nur al-Ilahi*, Divine Light. And when he was dressed with that Divine Light, from that very time, all things were opened to him; no veils remained. After that, the Prophet ﷺ was dressed from God's Ocean of Power, *Bahru 'l- Qudrah*.

The Prophet ﷺ therefore received three attributes as he came out from the Water of Life: First, he was washed with the Water of Light and given eternal Life. Second, he received Divine Light. Third, the Prophet ﷺ received the power from God's Ocean of Power.

At the second station, the Prophet ﷺ was with everyone, feeling with everyone. That is the meaning of the verse:

**Know that the Prophet is with you, among you, inside you.**[93]

because he was dressed with that Divine Light. That is why the Prophet ﷺ can know what you are feeling, what your future is, what you are doing, and what is going to happen both here and hereafter. God has given him that power.

What I am disclosing is from high knowledge and must be understood carefully. At the third station, the Prophet was granted the attribute of power from *Bahru 'l-Qudrah*, the Ocean of Power, which Moses ؏ had asked for and God did not give him. Moses ؏ asked God to give him from that Ocean of Power, to be able to say to something, "Be!" and it will be; God said, "No: but look at the mountain; I am going to send the light on that mountain. If the mountain remains, you will be given that power. If it melts or is destroyed, you cannot be given that power, for then you would melt also." When God sent that light to the mountain the mountain collapsed and Moses ؏ fell unconscious.[94] That is why God told him it was not for him, but for the last Prophet ﷺ.

God has given that Ocean of Power to the Prophet ﷺ, with which he can say to anything, "Be!" and it will be—without having to request God for permission, for he is swimming in that Ocean. The Prophet ﷺ said, "Whatever God has poured into my heart, I have poured into the heart of Abu Bakr as-Siddiq." Then Abu Bakr ؇ gave all that to Salman al-Farsi ؇; Salman to Qasim ؇, Qasim to Ja'far as-Sadiq ؇; Ja'far to Tayfur [Bistami] Tayfur ق, to Sayyidina Khidr ؏—and that secret is coming down to this day to

---

[93] Suratu 'l-Hujurat, 49:7. Arabic: *W'alamu anna feekum Rasulullah*.
[94] Cf. Suratu 'l-'Araf, 7:143.

Grandshaykh ق, and from Grandshaykh to Mawlana Shaykh Nazim ق.

When God has given something, He will not take it back. That is the meaning of generosity. When you give something, you do not take it back and you do not regret giving it; if you do, you are not generous. God gave this power to the Prophet ﷺ, to say, "BE!" to anything and it will be, and he is keeping it for the Last Day, in order to bring the whole Community to Paradise. The Prophet ﷺ is not going to leave anyone of the Community behind. He is going to take everyone by the hand and bring them to Paradise. Such is our Prophet ﷺ.

### Five Levels of the Heart

After these three attributes with which God adorned the Prophet ﷺ, come the five levels of the heart. As God dressed him, the Prophet's ﷺ heart was immediately endowed with the Divine Power of five positions of the heart, one after another, in quick succession. The first level is the Station of the Heart, *Qalb*; second is the Secret, *Sirr*; third, the Secret of the Secret, *Sirr as-sirr*; fourth the Hidden, *Khafa*, and fifth the Most Hidden, *Akhfa*.

Grandshaykh and Mawlana Shaykh Nazim said that after the Prophet ﷺ had been dressed with all these levels, whatever sins and bad manners come from this Community, even if the sins of every servant equal the number of the Community of the Prophet ﷺ (which, according to Sufi teachings, numbers 400 billion), for the Prophet ﷺ it is like something one cleans off with a little bit of water. Such is the light that God has given to the Prophet ﷺ, that he can clean all these sins for the benefit of this Community, as if nothing had happened. As the Prophet ﷺ said:

*My intercession is for the great sinners of my Community.*[95]

## The Best Community

This is the best Community that God has created as He said:

**Ye are the best community that hath been raised up for mankind.**[96]

and the Prophet ﷺ said:

*The best Community, the most favored Community, is the last Community.*

You are the last Community. According to Grandshaykh, this world has very little time left. After that, something is going to happen, the like of which you have never heard about, for the best of this world. Resurrection Day follows this by a short time. Through those mercies with which the Prophet ﷺ has been dressed, all sins of the Community are going to be removed.

## Hadith of the Great Intercession

Anas related that the Prophet Muhammad ﷺ spoke to the Companions, saying:

*On the Day of Resurrection the people will surge with each other like waves, and then they will come to Adam and say, "Please intercede for us with your Lord." He will say, "I am not fit for that; you better go to Abraham as he is the Friend of the Merciful." They will go to Abraham and he will say, "I am not fit for that; you better go to Moses as he is the one to whom God spoke directly." So they will go to Moses and he will say, "I am not fit for that; you better go to Jesus as he is a soul created by God and His Word, by saying,*

---

[95] Tirmidhi, Abu Dawud and Ibn Majah.
[96] Surat Ali 'Imran, 3:110.

'Be!' and it was." They will go to Jesus and he will say, "I am not fit for that; you better go to Muhammad."
They would come to me and I would say, "I am for that." Then I will ask for my Lord's permission, and it will be given, and then He will inspire me to praise Him with such praises as I do not know now. So I will praise Him with those praises and will fall down, prostrate before Him. Then it will be said, "O Muhammad, raise your head and speak, for you will be listened to; and ask, for your will be granted your request; and intercede, for your intercession will be accepted." I will say, "O Lord, my followers! My followers!" And then it will be said, "Go and take out of Hellfire all those who have faith in their hearts, equal to the weight of a barley grain." I will go and do so and return to praise Him with the same praises, and fall down prostrate before Him. Then it will be said, "O Muhammad, raise your head and speak, for you will be listened to, and ask, for you will be granted your request; and intercede, for your intercession will be accepted." I will say, "O Lord, my followers! My followers!" It will be said, "Go and take out of it all those who have faith in their hearts equal to the weight of a small ant or a mustard seed." I will go and do so and return to praise Him with the same praises, and fall down in prostration before Him. It will be said, "O, Muhammad, raise your head and speak, for you will be listened to, and ask, for you will be granted your request; and intercede, for your intercession will be accepted." I will say, "O Lord, my followers!" Then He will say, "Go and take out all those in whose hearts there is faith even to the lightest, lightest mustard seed. Take them out of the Fire." I will go and do so."'
I then return for a fourth time and praise Him similarly and prostrate before Him me the same as he "O Muhammad, raise your head and speak, for you will be listened to; and ask, for you will be granted your request; and intercede, for your intercession will be accepted." I will say, "O Lord, allow me to intercede for whoever said, "None has the right to be worshiped except God." Then God will say, "By my Power, and my Majesty, and by My Supremacy,

*and by My Greatness, I will take out of Hellfire whoever said, 'None has the right to be worshipped except God.'"*[97]

Grandshaykh said that even if every person has four hundred billion sins, they would be nothing; even if they were to number as God's creations, universes, and beings. Even then it remains easy for the Ocean of the Prophet ﷺ to remove all these sins—as if nothing had touched you.

Do not think that God has created this creation and left it just like that. God is going to dress His saints, and to dress the Prophet ﷺ from His Attributes and from His Lights in order to take everyone from miseries and sins to the highest levels in the hereafter.

## Salman, the Persian

Salman al-Farsi ؓ was a Companion of the Prophet ﷺ who was given the Prophet's inheritance from Sayyidina Abu Bakr as-Siddiq ؓ. He came from Persia. He knew from books and from extraordinary signs in the stars, that the last Prophet ﷺ was about to appear. He knew that there would be a very big incident in this world. In order to come to Makkah, he sold himself as a slave to people traveling to Makkah, and he walked the camel of the person who bought him over a thousand miles to Makkah, in order to meet the Prophet ﷺ. Now, we are reluctant to go even twenty or forty miles by car, saying it is too far. Look at the saints travelling vast distances, under arduous circumstances, in order to meet the Prophet ﷺ.

When the Prophet ﷺ was brought to this world by his mother, Sayyidina Salman al-Farsi ؓ heard the happiness of wild animals reciting the praise and glorification of God, for everyone in this universe was happy, including animals, trees and stars, at the arrival of last prophet, and everyone knew that God was going to

---

[97] Bukhari.

dress him with His Lights—all knew and were happy except us, human beings. Human beings are jealous of the Prophet ﷺ and say, "Why has God chosen him?"

Grandshaykh said, "I am speaking from that Ocean of Knowledge that is going to be opened when Mahdi ؏ is coming. The extent of the knowledge that I am revealing is like light that comes through the hole of a needle." If Mawlana is speaking as if from the hole of a needle, then what we are saying now is nothing compared to reality. What is going to come is something concerning which you are going to lose your minds. This is the explanation of Sayyidina Abu Hurayrah's ؓ affirmation:

> *The Prophet ﷺ has put in my heart two vessels of knowledge. One vessel I have disseminated amongst the people; but if I were to tell the other they would cut my throat.*

What Grandshaykh says is from the second knowledge—something extraordinary which is going to be spread in Mahdi's time.

## The Prophet's Heart is Washed

Grandshaykh said that these things have been opened on the heart of the Prophet ﷺ from the time of his birth and that his heart is like a glass of water, transparent from all sides. His heart was so transparent from the light of God that wherever the Prophet ﷺ looked, he could receive knowledge and wisdom, and therefore speak from that knowledge and wisdom.

Grandshaykh said that when the Prophet's ﷺ soul was taken away from his physical body by angels to the Presence of his Lord, just after his birth, his mother was afraid that he had passed away, because his body did not move for a full hour. But the angel Gabriel ؏ quickly came and said to her, "Don't be afraid, and don't tell anyone; leave it. God has taken his soul in order for his heart to be washed, and in order to open to him all the Oceans of all the ninety-nine Names and Attributes of God." According to the Islam, God has ninety-nine Names. Each Name covers an Attribute and each Attribute is an Ocean of Knowledge of unfathomable depth.

The Prophet's ﷺ heart was washed with God's Greatest Name Ismillah al-'Adham. Until today every saint is trying to discover the Greatest Name of God, but no one can know it, for that secret has not been opened to anyone yet, except to the Prophet ﷺ who has received that name in his heart. No veil was left on the heart of the Prophet ﷺ when his heart was washed with the river of Kawthar, the Paradise river God gave to the Prophet ﷺ when He said:

**We have given you (O Muhammad!) the Kawthar.**[98]

If anyone bathes in it, his heart will never die. That is why the Prophet ﷺ said:

*I am fresh, alive in my grave.*[99]

When he was only one hour old, the Prophet ﷺ asked God as his heart was being washed, "O my Lord, what about my Community? Aren't you going to wash my Community also with the water of this river? If not, I am not accepting to be washed alone. I must have my Community with me; I cannot be without my Community." According to the Prophet ﷺ, when he asked this from God, God washed all his Community with that River of Life. He washed them and cleaned their hearts until their hearts were clean and transparent like the Prophet's ﷺ, and He gave them to the Prophet ﷺ, "I am giving you your Community, clean, pure, lenient-hearted, soft-hearted, merciful, humble, loving and respecting each other. Are you taking them?" The Prophet ﷺ

---

[98] Suratu 'l-Kawthar, 108:1.
[99] "The Prophets are alive and they pray in their graves." (al-Mundhiri and al-Bayhaqi who classed it as authentic)

looked at all of them and saw them pure and clean and said, "I am accepting them."

When he ﷺ accepted them, then God showed him how much they are going to sin when they come to this world. The Prophet ﷺ said, "O my Lord, what have You done?" God said, "Never mind: light will never disappear from their hearts. They are going to dress that light with darkness; but it is going to be like a cloth, and I am giving you saints who will be your helpers, in order to polish their hearts and clean them."

## The Forgiven Community

We are a forgiven Community.[xxxii] God has entrusted us to the Prophet ﷺ with His Mercy. You are going to hear more and more of these lectures. Yet what we have said is child's play. When Grandshaykh gives permission to talk from such knowledge, these lectures are not for everyone to hear. They are special and that subject can only be opened with permission from Grandshaykh and Mawlana Shaykh Nazim.

After the Prophet ﷺ accepted his Community with all their light, and after God showed him the sins they were going to commit, the Prophet ﷺ asked for helpers. God immediately gave him 7,007 Naqshbandi saints to help him cleanse the Community. Out of these, He gave 313 a higher level. Out of these, He gave forty masters of the Golden Chain: our link to the Prophet ﷺ. Our forty masters are trying their best to clean everyone of their sins with the light that God has given to their hearts. You are lucky that you are in the hands of one of these masters—the last master in this chain, the fortieth master.

What is Kawthar? According to scriptural tradition it is a river in Paradise, but according to the Sufi understanding and knowledge, Kawthar is the name of one of the Grandshaykhs. That Grandshaykh, with the water that God symbolized by that name, can remove all the sins of every one of his followers, and present them clean to the Prophet ﷺ each night. That is why you must be happy that you have been connected to an eminent master of this Golden Chain.

Grandshaykh and our Master Shaykh Nazim asked, "Why has God given prophecy to the Prophet ﷺ? Is it just for him?" Grandshaykh is saying, "No: God has given that power and dressed him with the ninety-nine Names and Attributes and all this light, for the sake of this Community—in order that the Prophet ﷺ would dress each one of us with the same light and the same attributes, to share with us all these Attributes."

God has told the Prophet ﷺ, "O my beloved Prophet, I am going to ask you personally—I want everyone of this Community of my servants to be like you. If they are not going to be like you, I am not accepting you as a prophet." It is a great and tremendous secret that the Prophet ﷺ is under this responsibility: to make everyone of us, everyone of his Community, like him. He is going to share with us all of his worship; in order to clean and adorn us with all that he has been adorned, and to present us to God as clean as himself. This is his duty.

Grandshaykh and Mawlana Shaykh Nazim said, "In every blink of an eye the Prophet ﷺ is ascending a redoubled distance in the Presence of God, in growing geometrical sequence, each moment doubling the previous distance of progress—*yataraqqa mithlayni mithlayn*. He is progressing, and at the same time taking his Community by the hand with him—without discrimination and without differentiation. The Community is a community of servants, and servants are servants. There is no difference between servants! All of them are servants before God, and the Prophet ﷺ is looking at them as one, and taking them by the hand.

This knowledge is going to be opened in the time of Mahdi ؏ and Jesus ؏. Now this is only a whiff of the knowledge of what is going to happen later.

When others speak about Sufism, they are children in relation to what the Golden Chain is taking from the Prophet's ﷺ heart. What is going to be unveiled soon will dwarf what these people, who call themselves Sufi masters, are saying. They are going to find themselves as children. Their knowledge is nothing.

Sayyidina Muhyiddin Ibn 'Arabi ق, after writing *Al-Futuhat al-Makkiyyah* said, "I don't know what I wrote." He used to sleep with a pen by his side; when he woke up he found that the pen had written. That is also how he wrote *Fusus al-Hikam* and all his books. Even he did not understand, and now they are "explaining" what even he did not understand. What do they understand of what he said? This high degree of knowledge in Sufism cannot be opened, even if you think you see it: if you have a television you can see something but you do not feel. In Sufism, if you don't feel and live the event, you can never reach the level which is being described.

## Sufism is Taste

Sufism is *dhawq*—taste. You have many kinds of food. People take the best food, and they try to taste it from here [points to mouth] to here [points to top of throat]. After that point all foods are the same. Similarly, when you look at the television, it is as if "from here to here." You are not tasting or feeling anything. If you cannot feel or taste, it is not Sufism, but a mirror reflection of Sufism, an image. And all these "shaykhs"—they cannot be called by that title in fact, because to be a shaykh is a high level—all these people that are explaining Sufism, are neither tasting nor feeling. Yet feeling and tasting are the essential goal of Sufism.

## A Diamond for a Candy

Now you will say, "You are also speaking like them. Why are you not feeling and tasting?" I will tell you that there is not yet permission to take you by the hand and make you taste and feel. This is only when Mahdi ﷺ comes; otherwise, this world could not carry you. If you give a child a candy, he would trade a diamond for it and lose the diamond. If you are going to be given such knowledge, you are going to waste it if there is no support from Mahdi ﷺ. That support is needed. Without it, you will never have the door of feeling and tasting opened for you. We hope Mahdi ﷺ appears soon and that support is given.

## Three Levels of Certainty

A Sufi leader must have the Knowledge of Certainty, the Certainty of Vision, the Reality of Certainty.[100] First, is the Knowledge of Certainty, which is the necessity to know that there is such knowledge and to hear about it. When you hear it, you ascend to the second level, but first you must hear it. That is why God in Qur'an, as well as all the Sufi masters, from Jalaluddin Rumi to Ibn 'Arabi ق, to Hallaj ق, to Bayazid al-Bistami ق, mention hearing as the first sense. Knowledge cannot come by seeing first, but from a teacher that is heard, even for a blind man. A deaf person, on the other hand, cannot as easily begin to acquire knowledge. When the archangel Gabriel ﷺ came to the Prophet ﷺ, the first thing he said to him was, *"Read!"* and the Prophet ﷺ was hearing and listening. That is why Sufism is giving orders which one fulfills by hearing, not by seeing.

This first level is not achieved by hearing and ignoring, but by hearing, accepting and fulfilling through action! If your shaykh says to go to California, stand by the ocean, and throw yourself in, and you do not do it, you are still considered a child in Sufi knowledge. In the Naqshbandi order you have to obey, and obedience comes through hearing. If you do it, then you can go to the second level.

---

[100] Arabic respectively: 'Ilmu 'l-Yaqeen, 'Aynu 'l-Yaqeen, Haqqu 'l-Yaqeen.

Once, Grand-Grandshaykh Sharafuddin ق was sitting in a meeting of big masters in a remote place far outside the city. Grandshaykh 'Abd Allah, who was Shaykh Sharafuddin's disciple—still a teenager at the time—was on his way to meet them. Seeing him approaching from afar, Shaykh Sharafuddin told the assembled masters:

> My son 'Abd Allah Effendi has reached a level where no one has set foot yet—not myself, nor all the Golden Chain masters. He is only eighteen, and I am sixty, yet he has reached a level that is higher than mine and all the Golden Chain masters that have passed away. If I am going to send him a child of seven years to tell him, "Your shaykh is ordering you to direct yourself to Makkah for pilgrimage," from Daghestan here in the middle of Russia, he will immediately think, without coming and asking me for confirmation whether this is true or not, "Who is making that child speak? My shaykh has to know even before I know. Otherwise, how have I accepted him as a shaykh and yet represent him as not knowing anything? If my shaykh doesn't know, who will know?" Immediately he will believe the child, and without going back to his house to tell his mother or his wife that he wants to go to pilgrimage; without taking any clothes, money, or food, he will direct himself to Makkah which is 10,000 miles away, walking, without asking anything. He will know the order comes from me and will simply change the direction of his walk.

This is level is known as the Unification of Actions (*Wahdatu 'l-af'al*)—you must see everything as coming from God. This is a higher level in Sufi knowledge. You cannot see people doing anything anymore, but you must consider them instruments in the Hands of God. Leave the child—if Shaykh Nazim comes to you and says, "Go to Makkah," you will say, "Okay, my shaykh, but I have to buy a ticket, and I have to see if my wife gives me permission..." In the Naqshbandi order you cannot do all this. You have to move immediately.

The second level is the Certainty of Vision—*'Aynu 'l-Yaqeen*. At that time you are going to see things around you, but without feeling. It will be like a screen which is lifted only in the third level, the Reality of Certainty—*Haqqu 'l-Yaqeen*—in which you are there and living that incident. If Grandshaykh is saying what we were saying before about the Prophet ﷺ, how he was taken and how his heart was washed, on hearing this, you are going to live that event as if you were living and feeling everything at that time. If Mawlana Shaykh Nazim is talking about an incident which happened five hundred years ago, for example, you are going to experience it as if you were living at that time, hearing, seeing and feeling what they were hearing, seeing and feeling, just as if you were one of them.

This is the Sufi taste and the knowledge of the Naqshbandi order which connects its seekers to the Golden Chain. This cannot be opened until the time of Mahdi ﷺ—unless, for some special followers, Mawlana Shaykh Nazim opens it with permission from the Prophet ﷺ. It is not common to all. The rest must wait for the support of Mahdi's spiritual power to enter that level, otherwise people might be regarded as heretics for speaking about what they see.

In the Naqshbandi order the shaykh can never make you be different from people and this is the perfect order: you see the shaykh who has all this power, feeling everything and living all the events, and describing them, yet behaving as an ordinary person. In other Sufi orders they could not control themselves: they began talking and were rejected by the people. The shaykh will, therefore, never accept to open knowledge for you if you are not ready, and if he sees that you are going to show what he gave you to the public. That is why there is no permission yet for that door to be opened.

# The Three Lights of Humankind

The title of every lecture is:

> *Obey God, obey the Prophet, and obey those in authority among you.*[101]

By obeying the Prophet ﷺ, you are obeying God. We have mentioned that Grandshaykh and Mawlana Shaykh Nazim, may God bless their secret, said that when the Prophet ﷺ was born, angels took his soul and washed it with the Light of God, the Water of Life. One of God's Holy Names is Al-Hayy, the Living One. From the attribute of that Name, God ordered angels to wash the spirit of the Prophet ﷺ. Then God dressed him from the Ocean of Power and gave him the power of the five levels of the heart, which are found in every person: the Stations of Heart; Secret; Secret of the Secret; Hidden; and Most Hidden. When these levels were opened to the Prophet ﷺ, they came with the support of the Light of God, *an-Nuru 'l-ilahi*, a special light the outpouring of which is referred to indirectly in the verse:

> *Know that the Prophet is within you*[102]

for were it not for that light of God inside each one of us, we could never be alive, but would be dead instead. The meaning of that power that God dressed the Prophet ﷺ with is that the Prophet ﷺ is in everyone of us.

---

[101] Suratu 'n-Nisa, 4:59.
[102] Suratu 'l-Hujurat, 49:7.

This knowledge is not found in Divine Law (*Shari'ah*) [Islamic law], but nevertheless Divine Law must be observed rigorously in all things. Do not claim, as some groups do, "We don't need Divine Law"—no. Divine Law is a must in order to follow Sufism. This said, God willing we shall now pick up where we left off yesterday.

## The Oceans of Divine Names

Mawlana Shaykh Nazim says that the Prophet ﷺ did not ascend into the presence of God only once, on the night of the 27th of Rajab, during the Ascension, but from the very first day he was born and from the first hour, the Prophet ﷺ was taken by angels to be dressed by God with the Oceans of the ninety-nines Names, each name of which is an Ocean. He was dressed with all this knowledge from the first moment he was born. By dressing him with the Divine Names, God has given the Prophet ﷺ a special power and a special knowledge that no human can reach. That is why he was illiterate and came from a desert where no one knows how to read and write, yet brought all these different kinds of knowledge. It is something amazing to bring something like the Holy Qur'an, in imitation of which no one can write even one verse, such is its beauty, surpassing the purest poetry ever heard.

Mawlana Shaykh Nazim said that God gave the Prophet ﷺ this power not for himself, but for his Community—for us. That power and knowledge were given to the Prophet ﷺ for his Community. And who is his Community? Do you think it is us? *All* human beings are the Community of the Prophet ﷺ, for God said to Adam ﷺ the father of human beings, "If Muhammad ﷺ came in your time you would be following him," and in the holy Qur'an:

> *We did not send you [O Muhammad] except as a mercy for all creation.*[103]

He did not say "for your Community," but "for human beings." The Prophet ﷺ was therefore given this power from God for the human race. There are infinite creations of God's that we don't know about. When you pass away, at that time you are awake and you know what God has created in other universes. In this life you can never know what the other creations are, where they are living, and what they are doing, except if you are able to open the eyes of the heart. This is done progressively and through the way of our master, Shaykh Muhammad Nazim al-Haqqani ق. That is the path we believe in, and the only one we can follow in order to find that reality. Without it nothing will ever be found.

When connected to the energy in a current a bulb keeps giving light until it burns out. If our hearts are burnt out and stop working, light can no longer be found in them. One must therefore keep the eye of the heart open, in order to see what these physical eyes cannot see. Then this burning can be prevented. God said in Qur'an:

> *Verily We have honored the children of Adam.*[104]

How did He honor them? And once He honored them, will He take it back? If a generous person gives you something, will he take it back from you? God called the Prophet ﷺ and said, "O my beloved Prophet, I have created human beings from three lights. These lights can never be darkened." Mawlana Shaykh Nazim is describing how God honored human beings: by giving them these three lights; lights which can never be darkened by the sins we are committing.

---

[103] Suratu 'l-Anbiya, 21:107.
[104] Suratu 'l-Isra, 17:70.

Mawlana Shaykh Nazim said that this knowledge is from the heart of Mahdi ﷺ. This knowledge will only be opened fully when Mahdi ﷺ comes; now you can only scent a whiff, like fragrant perfume from a distance.

The first is the Light of God. When God created human beings, He ordered the angel Gabriel ﷺ to go to earth and bring some clay. When he brought the clay, God looked at it with His light, and mixed the clay with His light. The second is the light of the Prophet ﷺ, whose name was written next to God's Name at the "pre-beginning" of creation, when God ordered the Pen to write *"La ilaha ill-Allah Muhammadun Rasulullah*—There is no god except Allah and Muhammad is the Prophet of God."

The third the light came from our father, Adam ﷺ. God mixed Adam's light with his clay, and that is why all generations came from him, and God told him, "O Adam, if the Prophet was born in your time, you would follow him. Do not say that you are his father, therefore, because he is your father spiritually."

Human beings are from those three lights: one light from God, one light from the Prophet ﷺ and one light from Adam ﷺ. God told the Prophet ﷺ, "O Prophet, as there is no change for my Greatness, there will be no change for that honor that I gave human beings." All human beings are therefore of the same level and position in the presence of God. This is all coming from the secret of that verse in Holy Qur'an, **"We have honored human beings."** Even if we claim distinction, nowadays, by saying, "These are believers; those are unbelievers"—this judgment belongs to your Lord. Don't talk about another's bad manners, or disbelief, or innovation; it is not your business. Our business is to keep these three lights clean. We don't like these three lights to be stained, just like clothes, because you are going to be ashamed before your Lord later.

We must be very happy for having such a merciful Lord. If these secrets are going to be spread they would make all this world as nothing. This is a drop in the ocean of the knowledge of saints, which is a drop in the ocean of the knowledge of the Prophet ﷺ, and the knowledge of the Prophet ﷺ is like a drop in comparison to the knowledge of God. This is a drop in the ocean of the knowledge of Mawlana Shaykh Nazim. Do not think too much of what you are hearing. When Mawlana Shaykh Nazim is going to place only one drop of his heart's knowledge into your heart you will be flying.

For this reason in the circle of saints Mahdi ؑ said that if there was no support from God he would never come out with this knowledge: everyone would oppose him for revealing it. Saints are therefore waiting for Mahdi ؑ because they need his spiritual power to support them when they reveal this knowledge. If anyone rejects what they bring, at that time Mahdi ؑ will deal with them.

## Knowledge of the Naqshbandiyya

The knowledge of the Naqshbandi order is the highest knowledge that can ever be imagined. This knowledge is taken from the heart of Sayyidina Abu Bakr as-Siddiq ؓ according to the Prophet's ﷺ saying that he put into Abu Bakr's heart everything that God had put into his own heart; and all saints of the Naqshbandi order are taking from the heart of Abu Bakr as-Siddiq ؓ.

## Can God Curse His Creation?

Mawlana Shaykh Nazim said that, "God has cursed tyrants and unbelievers."

Now we are going to say something big—be careful. Mawlana asked: In what circumstances did this curse that God has pronounced on tyrants and unbelievers come about? It came through the Holy Book, but on what tongue? Who brought the Holy Qur'an? Who recited it? From whom did the Companions ؓ listen to it? From God? No, but from the Prophet ﷺ. Therefore it is according to that level, on the tongue of the Prophet ﷺ, that God is cursing tyrants and unbelievers.

Above that level, at the level of His Majesty and His Presence, "Do you think," Mawlana asks, "that there is such a curse?" God has honored humankind—how could He be cursing them? But God is talking, through the Holy Qur'an, to us, and through the tongue of the Prophet ﷺ, as a human being. The Prophet ﷺ is a human being, and God is God—we are worshipping God, and no other than our Lord. What came on the tongue of a human being, therefore, came for human beings. But above that level, in the presence of God, after God has honored those human beings with these three lights, do you think He could then be cursing these lights?

This physical body is nothing. There is no consideration owed this physical body. What is all-important is the light God has dressed this form with. Do you think there is a curse on such a light? If there were, then God has been harmed: a human being curses one that has harmed him. But God is Greater. He does not endure pain, suffering or dishonor as human beings do: why curse humans then? He honored us with His honor, and said that just as His Greatness did not change, our honor would not change. That curse came on the tongue of the Prophet ﷺ, therefore, to try as much as possible to keep us on the right path in this life.

That knowledge, Mawlana Shaykh Nazim said, comes from the heart of the Prophet ﷺ and was revealed in the association of the saints. That is from the second vessel of knowledge given to the Companions ؓ and alluded to by Sayyidina Abu Hurayrah ؓ when he said, "If I spread this knowledge they would cut my throat." We are getting a little bit of that knowledge now. These secrets are going to be opened little by little, slowly, by God's leave, until Mawlana gives permission to open more and more knowledge.

Human beings are all of them are made from the Light of God, from the Light of the Prophet ﷺ, and from the Light of Adam ﷺ. That holy light is always with them. That is why it is unacceptable for any one to curse another human being. The only One who may judge servants is the Lord of servants. Otherwise, why did the Prophet ﷺ say, "The heart of a believer is the house of God?"[105] If God has taken the heart of a human being as the locus of revelation, how can He at the same time scold a human being? It is impossible, but He scolded human beings, in the person of unbelievers, only on the tongue of the Prophet ﷺ and at our level, so that we would understand. Just as we instill fear from us on our children's part sometimes to teach them not to fail, also God, through the Qur'an, which is brought on the tongue of the Prophet ﷺ, to keep human beings on the right path and follow the correct way of life and the right path and to encourage people to worship Him and believe in Him and to be spiritual, following the messages of His prophets.

## Angelic Voices

On the night of his rapture to the Divine Presence, when the Prophet ﷺ entered the seventh heaven, what he saw surpassed all imagination and all recorded books, all fabled accounts, all legends and all histories.

Silent gold sat on stars of pearl. Under every pearl, fifty thousand angels whirled in a lake of galaxies, producing a heavenly sound like a million million birds humming on top of the buzzing of a million million bees. Everything was moving at the speed of light, but at the same time everything was silent and still. Each angel spoke words of greetings to the Prophet ﷺ at the

---

[105] Ghazzali, Suhrawardi.

same time in a different language, but distinctly and without any clash one with the other. Their words were phrased in diadems and garlands of light, which he wore one after the other on his head and around his neck. A huge angel named Semla'il appeared at the head of 10,000 processions of similar angels, wearing a crown of multi-colored garnets and reciting praise of God in an angelic language which made each angel swoon and rise up in turn. These were the Cherubim (Qarubiyyun), "Those Brought Near." No-one on earth can see them and live because of the intensity of their light which they borrow from the One they behold.

The Prophet ﷺ asked Gabriel, "O Gabriel! What is this untarnished heavenly sound?" Gabriel answered, "O Prophet of God, this is the music of the angelic souls in the Presence of their Lord, trembling like a leaf, not daring to move or speak, awed and annihilated by perfection, yet vivified and moved by Divine Light, rushing to the Divine Meeting to announce your coming."

The movements of angels in this universe has an influence on the states of human beings on this earth. From the movements of these angels, by God's order, the connection is made between the movements of galaxies. The transmission of signals even millions of light-years away from us affects the states of human nature. The heavenly world thus, always holds sway over the earthly world.

Everything is created in hierarchies and everything is connected to what is above it. Human beings always look up, not down. The desire for betterment is built into them at both the material and the spiritual levels. The principle of the heavenly influences is founded upon this: the effect of the upward on the downward, and the aspiration of the downward to the upward.

## Have You Heard the Qur'an?

Our Grandshaykh says, "The only one who heard the Qur'an truly was the Prophet ﷺ. Only he has heard the real sound of the revelation from God. People, however, have heard the sound from the Prophet ﷺ. And we heard it on the tongue of the Prophet ﷺ."

When the Prophet ﷺ approached his Lord, with what sound and what voice did God speak to him? The Prophet ﷺ heard the Holy Qur'an as a revelation with a sound that is heavenly, and therefore undescribable in this world. That leads us to say, what kind of a sound; have he heard such a sound? That will lead us to ask, is there a language special for the Prophet ﷺ; is there a language special for saints? Is there a language special for the human race? That indescribable heavenly language, leaves us stunned when we begin to ponder the spiritual dimension of its sound and what it produces of different wavelengths in the heavenly atmosphere, compared to sounds and voices that are produced by wavelengths in the atmosphere of this world. So when someone reaches that high angelic spiritual source, indeed the sounds will change to his ear.

What the Prophet ﷺ recited was what he heard from God and gave to us, but what God had really given of secrets to the Prophet ﷺ, no one knows. In the Judgment Day, God is going to read Surat al-An'am by Himself—at that time, all human beings, even saints, and even the Prophet ﷺ, are going to fall unconscious from the sweetness of hearing God's Voice.

People look at the heart as a piece of flesh. In fact, this heart is made up of five levels or stations. Moses ﷺ tried with all his power to know the Greatest Name of God (*Ismillah al-'adham*). By asking to "see" God, Moses ﷺ meant that he wanted to know the Greatest Name of God.[xxxiii] This can never be known in this world. How can God come to something created? Something created cannot encompass the Creator, for the creation is limited while the Creator is unlimited. How will the limited encompass the unlimited? That is why God cannot appear in this world, and no one can see Him.

But one can know the secret of the Greatest Name. Yet Moses ﷺ was not able to do so. God told him it was impossible; He told him to look at the mountain while His gaze set upon it: if that mountain stood still, Moses ﷺ would have come to know God's secret; if not, he could never know it. And when Moses ﷺ looked at that mountain, the mountain dissolved.

God's Greatest Name is engraved on the heart of human beings. However, it needs someone who has the power and the secret of the Greatest Name to bring it out. This also needs the support of the spiritual power of Mahdi ﷺ. Without that support, saints are not allowed to open the secret of that Name.

## The Safety of Sham

In Mahdi's time there will be no more safety in the entire world except in one place: Sham (Damascus). Only in that place will there be safety to be found. According to the Prophet ﷺ:

> *When confusion and seditions appear, safety is in Sham.*[106]

Sedition, confusion and war will be spread throughout this world except in Sham, because five groups of spiritual beings—*Budala, Nujaba, Nuqaba, Awtad, Akhyar*—are going to erect barricades around it in order that whoever is inside remains safe. They are waiting for Mahdi ﷺ to give them the signal.

What we are speaking about now is in preparation for that day. If you live to see that era, all of you are going to find yourselves there at that time, by the power of your shaykh. By reciting "*Bismillahi 'r-Rahmani 'r-Rahim*—in the name of God, the

---

[106] *Musnad* Ahmad Ibn Hanbal.

Merciful, the Compassionate," you will find yourself there. No need for planes, cars or ships, just spiritual power.

You have to be warned: don't try to evaluate the words and knowledge of saints. No one can evaluate that high knowledge: it is a standard that can never be reached. Do not, therefore, try to pierce it with your mind: you would be a *fasiq*, a transgressor, just as those who tried to judge the words of Muhyiddin Ibn 'Arabi ق became transgressors for their rejectin. He was speaking from a standpoint of high knowledge, as when saints do when they want to open something. We could not go higher than what we are saying now, because your minds could not bear it. Then one would become a *fasiq*. That is why this scent is sometimes given: you have to know that there is secret knowledge hidden from you, such as you have never heard before.

The Prophet ﷺ ordered Bilal to make the call to prayer (*adhan*) one night to summon all the Companions to his presence. When they all came in the dead of night, they were afraid about what they should expect to hear. The Prophet ﷺ said:

> The angel Gabriel ؏ came to me and told me that, in the last days of my Community in this world, there is a big valley by the name of Amuq (between Turkey and Syria), deep and flat, where a very big war is going to occur. Blood will be flowing so profusely that it will be able to sweep away a two-year old cow in its flow. You are going to see this event.

This is an example of how you can become a transgressor: if you evaluate the words of saints with your mind.

Despite hearing this hadith, the Companions ؓ never saw that incident. But to whom is the Prophet ﷺ talking through the Companions ؓ? We are the children of the Companions ؓ: this generation. The Prophet ﷺ was talking to the Companions while looking and knowing that from them, their children would come and see those events. He was therefore talking to the souls in the sperm that would carry the generations descending from the Companions ﷺ. The Prophet ﷺ knew even by individual name, at that time, who was going to come from their descendants, who going to see this and who not. Not all will see, only some. God willing, we hope to be among those who see these events in Mahdi's time.

Mawlana Shaykh said, "One night, I was praying to my Lord, 'O my Lord, open that door for Mahdi ﷺ to come out! This world is now a terrible world. Bad manners are everywhere; everyone has bad characters. No one is keeping the three lights You gave them to honor them. Everyone is running after his pleasure! Therefore, please open that door for Mahdi ﷺ.' I saw Mahdi ﷺ appearing in front of me and saying, 'I am very thankful for your prayer, O my brother, for it was the key for my door to be opened. I am going to be appearing, first for saints, then for all people.'"

This happened long ago. Mahdi ﷺ was a child when Mawlana Shaykh Nazim was making that prayer. He is waiting for God's signal ordering him to appear. He is going to appear, first in Madinah, then in Sham.

# The Ocean of Shah Naqshband

*O ye who believe! Obey God, obey the Prophet, and those in authority among you.*[107]

This verse must be obeyed in doing what they tell us and in following the way they show us. We believe that we are in need of guidance to show us the way—not as some are saying nowadays, that we have no such need. As God gave the Prophet ﷺ a guide on the Night Journey and Ascension (Laylat al-Isra' wa 'l-M'iraj), in the person of Archangel Gabriel ؈. As the angel Gabriel ؈ was the guide for the Prophet ﷺ to approach the presence of his Lord, so too do we need a guide to show us the way to approach the Prophet ﷺ, and then the Prophet ﷺ will show us the way to approach our Lord.

We do not care what some people say or do not say: We are opening in these lectures, following Mawlana Shaykh Nazim's order to us, some of the Sufi treasures of inner knowledge and spirituality. We are not going to wait to see if this person is accepting or if that person is objecting. We spend a lot of time teaching from Divine Law (*Shari'ah*); but this is some of the teachings of Reality (*haqiqah*). I repeat: Reality without Divine Law is not acceptable. We have to uphold Divine Law in all our behavior and all our manners. Divine Law will teach us discipline. We have to follow it for our physical discipline, and we have to follow the Path (*tariqah*) for our spiritual discipline.

We hope God does not leave us, as He left Moses ؈ in the desert of Sinai for forty years. He promised Moses ؈ to bring him

---

[107] Suratu 'n-Nisa, 4:59.

and his people to the Promised Land. For forty years God left him in the desert and told him, every night, "Tomorrow, tomorrow." The next day came and nothing happened. God was looking at his servants with the name As-Sabur, the Patient One. With that Name, He is looking at every servant. He is not looking at his servants with the name Al-Jabbar, the Forceful One. He is looking at us with the Names of mercy, Ar-Rahman, Ar-Rahim, and with the attribute of Patience. That is why He was also patient with Pharoah. Mawlana Shaykh Nazim said that God created everyone because He loved everyone. If He loves everyone He wants everyone to believe in Him. That is why He is patient, until the last moment. Perhaps we will remember and ask forgiveness, and enter God's paradise.

### The Reason for the Existence of Saints

That is why God has created saints. After Prophet Muhammad ﷺ there are no more prophets. He is the last one. But God gave the secret that He put in his heart to his Companions, and his Companions gave this secret to the saints. And this world, according to our Master, will never be devoid of such saints. If one dies he is immediately replaced. There are 124,000 living saints, as there have been 124,000 prophets, and 124,000 Companions. These saints have been given as a gift to the Prophet ﷺ in order to clean us from sins. One of these saints is Sayyidina Shah an-Naqshband. The following story will help us understand the greatness of this saint after whom our order is named.

After Prophet ﷺ the Naqshbandi order was entrusted to Sayyidina Abu Bakr as-Siddiq ؓ; after Abu Bakr as-Siddiq ؓ it was passed to Sayyidina Salman al-Farsi ؓ; after Sayyidina Salman it was passed to Sayyidina Qasim ؓ, the grandson of Sayyidina Abu Bakr as-Siddiq ؓ; from Sayyidina Qasim it was passed to Sayyidina Ja'far as-Sadiq ؑ, the grandson of Sayyidina al-Husayn ؑ; after Sayyidina Ja'far as-Sadiq ؑ it was passed to Sayyidina

Bayazid al-Bistami ق, sixth in the chain about four hundred years before Sayyidina Shah Naqshband ق.

## The Ocean of Shah Naqshband

Sayyidina Bayazid ق spent his whole life in struggling against his ego to uplift himself, seeking God's Face. He finally arrived at a level where he was in front of the Door to the Divine Presence. Sayyidina Bayazid ق was knocking at the door, asking to enter. At that time, God told him, "O Bayazid, you cannot enter My Divine Presence before you learn how to approach Me." Bayazid said, "O my Lord, teach me how to approach You." God said, "Be humble. Be a garbage dump for My servants and for all human beings."

Sayyidina Bayazid ق made himself so humble that he became a "garbage dump" for people. Scholars in his time decided to kill him. At that time he left his village and went to the sea-shore and found a ship sailing for another country. He boarded it and the ship left shore. There arose a big storm in the middle of the sea, ready to founder the ship and sink it. Bayazid prayed and asked his Lord, "O my Lord, if You are making this ship sink because of my sins, I am ready to throw myself into this ocean." He threw himself overboard and the ocean became still.

Sayyidina Bayazid ق sacrificed himself so that the people would remain alive; he carried their sins with him and took their punishment on himself. When Bayazid was inside the ocean, he swore that he would never come out again until he found truth and reality, and he decided to go, as mentioned in the Qur'an down to the "seventh earth" in order to find reality and bring it out for human beings.[108] He was moving through the water with unimaginable speed, moving from one layer of darkness to another. At the end, he was entering from one ocean of knowledge to another; an ocean of knowledge about this entire

---

[108] Cf. Suratu 't-Talaq, 65:12.

universe. At last he reached a place where he was hearing a sound like HUUUUU... as when someone places a seashell or some other object on their ear. That is the noise of the river of Kawthar in heaven, the movement or flowing of water that we can hear in our ears.<sup>xxxiv</sup>

Sayyidina Bayazid ق arrived at a place where he could hear that sound. He was astonished and wanted to know who was causing that voice. Mawlana said that Sayyidina Bayazid ق, with the power and light that God had given to his heart, could know and recite in less than five minutes the name of all human beings that God had created on this earth, each with their father's and mother's names without missing a single one, from the first man, Adam ؑ and first woman Eve, to the last person to live before Judgment Day. He used this power at that time in order to know how many people there were in that spot reciting this sound.

The name Hu is the Absolute Unseen, God's Unknowable Essence. God says in Qur'an:

### *Say: HU "He" is God, the Only One.*[109]

HU therefore refers to God, and this is in the *'ilmu 'l-ghayb*, the knowledge of the Unseen which no one can know. No one can know about that ocean and its meaning. Mawlana said that Sayyidina Bayazid ق used all that power that God gave to him trying to find out how many people were there reciting this: he kept trying, not for five minutes, but for seventy days, and he was still unable to count the number of people who were reciting in that location so great was their number. He then used his power trying to find out the name of the teacher who was teaching them to say this, and he found that it was Shah Naqshband ق.

---

[109] Suratu 'l-Ikhlas, 112:1.

Sayyidina Bayazid ق knew that that saint was going to come after him by ten saints in the lineage which begins with Sayyidina Abu Bakr as-Siddiq ؓ, five hundred years later; it was his spirit teaching the spirits of these people in that place. Mawlana Shaykh Nazim ق said that these people are from this world and from other planets that are under the Naqshbandi order. Do not think that we are under the Naqshbandi order only on this planet. Shah Naqshband ق is also responsible for other planets and he is teaching them.

When Bayazid al-Bistami ق discovered that Shah Naqshband ق was their teacher, he was afraid in his heart that Shah Naqshband ق would tell him, "Why are you interfering with my students? Why are you coming in a territory that is not yours?" Immediately he turned back from that ocean, the ocean of Shah Naqshband, the leader of the Naqshbandi order which we are following. Sayyidina Shah Naqshband ق is our teacher and he was given that great secret in his heart; he has passed it to his successors and it is coming down through them to our shaykh, Shaykh Muhammad Nazim al-Haqqani ق. It is from that secret knowledge that we are talking about Shah Naqshband ق.

When God gave Shah Naqshband ق that power, and told him that he was going to be a helper to the Prophet ﷺ in helping people repent from their sins, he asked one thing from the Prophet ﷺ. He said, "O my beloved Prophet, if you want me to be a helper, I need one thing from you. I have to be responsible for the angel on the right shoulder and the angel on the left shoulder of every human being in your communtiy. If you give me that responsibility, I am accepting the task." After the Prophet ﷺ asked his Lord and got this permission for Shah Naqshband ق, the latter accepted to be responsible for this Community.

Mawlana says:

Whenever someone sins, Shah Naqshband ق tries to send to the heart of that sinner the inspiration to seek forgiveness from his Lord. If the sinner does not ask forgiveness in twenty-four hours, before the time of the pre-dawn prayer, Shah Naqshband ق will ask forgiveness on behalf of that follower, and a reward will be written on the shoulder of that follower.

## The Farthest Limit

On the night of the Ascension, the night that the Prophet ﷺ went to the presence of his Lord in the company of Archangel Gabriel ؏, when he ﷺ reached the seventh heaven, Archangel Gabriel ؏ told him, "O Prophet of God, I cannot move further with you. This is my limit. If I go forward, I will be burnt." The Prophet ﷺ was moving alone to the presence of his Lord.

What the Prophet ﷺ gained and took from knowledge after that, Archangel Gabriel ؏ knew nothing about. If he was not able to know what the Prophet ﷺ took from God, how was he able to bring Qur'an to the Prophet ﷺ? Archangel Gabriel ؏ stood in a place and he was unable to move upwards; he said to the Prophet ﷺ, "You go alone to the presence of our Lord." The Prophet ﷺ was progressing alone after that. What he has gained from the level of Archangel Gabriel ؏ to the level of God, Mawlana Shaykh said that the Prophet ﷺ has moved approaching his Lord by passing five layers, the length of which was each of 500,000 years, and the years of God are not to be counted as our years:

> ***Verily a Day in the sight of thy Lord is like a thousand years of your reckoning.*** [110]

What kinds of wisdom and knowledge has the Prophet ﷺ seen there? This, no one knows. This knowledge is especially for the Prophet ﷺ. He is keeping that knowledge for the time when every one of the Community will be taken to Paradise. We are not caring

---

[110] Suratu'l-Hajj, 22:47.

for anyone who might say "yes" or "no": the Prophet ﷺ has given the knowledge gained above the level of Archangel Gabriel ؏ to the heart of saints, and the knowledge gained from below the level of Archangel Gabriel ؏ has been placed in the Divine Law (*Shari'ah*). This is the difference between Divine Law, and reality (*haqiqah*). That is the meaning of that hadith of Sayyidina Abu Hurayrah ؓ about the two knowledges, "The Prophet ﷺ has put in my heart two kinds of knowledge. One knowledge I explained to everyone"—this is Divine Law, the knowledge below Archangel Gabriel's level, "but if I express the other knowledge, they will cut my throat," is the knowledge above Archangel Gabriel's level.

That is also the difference between the people that accept this knowledge and those that deny it. How can they deny this knowledge? No one can deny the knowledge that the Prophet ﷺ has gained from above the level of Archangel Gabriel ؏.

When the Prophet ﷺ approached the presence of God, he saw a big lion and became afraid. God asked him, "O my beloved Prophet, what has made you afraid in this world?" He answered, "O my Lord, I have never been afraid in my life except from that lion that is in your presence." Mawlana Shaykh Nazim ق says that even the Prophet ﷺ did not receive all of God's knowledge. If he knew absolutely everything from God, he would never have been afraid of this lion. This means that the Prophet's ﷺ knowledge had still not reached its maximum. That is why the Prophet ﷺ is progressing forever, even in his grave, in approaching the presence of his Lord. Had he not been afraid, he would have known at that very time the secrets of "the knowledge of the beginnings, and the knowledge of the endings,"[111] but this belongs to God alone.

---

[111] Arabic: 'ulumu 'l-'awwalin wa 'l-akhireen.

The knowledge that the Prophet ﷺ has gained in his constant state of ascension, however, is going to be opened up when Mahdi ؑ comes. It cannot be opened now because it needs support. Without the support of Mahdi ؑ to support the saint that is going to reveal this knowledge, they will hang him, as Abu Hurayrah warned. You can see that many Sufi shaykhs in Islamic history have been hung for revealing such knowledge. Without the support of Mahdi ؑ, there is no permission for anyone to talk about such knowledge.

Now we are only smelling a whiff of that knowledge, like small drops seeping out to us in order to make everyone understand that there is a spiritual knowledge kept in hearts, and that this knowledge is going to be spread in everyone's heart when Mahdi ؑ comes. Before he comes, however, everyone can smell this knowledge. Those who want to smell have to attend associations of *dhikr*, without which they can never hear about this knowledge. It is a very high knowledge for everyone—both speaker and audience are listening. It cannot be covered in one, five or even ten lectures.

## An Ecstatic Utterance of Bayazid

If I say one word from Bayazid al-Bistami ق, of what he said to his Lord, people will call us unbelievers (*kafir*). It is true that if we say this word, we are unbelievers; but if Bayazid al-Bistami ق says it, he is a believer. He says it because he knows it, feels it and sees it. But if we say it, we would not be seeing it and feeling it, therefore we would be unbelievers—this is the difference.[xxxv]

Bayazid al-Bistami ق said, "O my Lord, my kingdom is greater than Yours."[112]

---

[112] Arabic: Mulki akbaru min mulkik.

What is the meaning of this utterance? He is telling his Lord, "O my Lord, You have created this universe, and You have said that this universe did not have, in Your eyes, the value of a gnat's wing, 'This universe is not worth a mosquito's wing in the sight of God.'[113] This means that this kingdom has no value; my kingdom, on the other hand, is You! You are my kingdom, and You are everything. That is why my kingdom is better than Your kingdom. Your kingdom is us, and we are nothing! But You are our kingdom, and You are everything. Ours, therefore, is better."

If we say this with our understanding, it is not acceptable. If Bayazid is saying it, he means it—we cannot mean it. The hadith of Sayyidina Abu Hurayrah inferred many such hidden things. This knowledge is restricted to saints. Praise God, that you believe in *awliya*, and this is the best and most important belief, after belief in God and belief in the Prophet ﷺ. And we are believing in Divine Law (*Shari'ah*). We must keep the Divine Law (*Shari'ah*) as the Prophet ﷺ showed us. And we cannot deny saints who are helpers and guides for us to purify our hearts and cleanse them of this materialistic life.

---

[113] Narrated by as-Suyuti.

# The Intercession of Saints

We must be happy. At no time must we be sad. God has created you. If He had not created you, you would never be existing. Always be happy and satisfied with the condition that God has put you in. Never object, despite whatever you see in this life. If you see it in a good way, you find it good. If you look at it in a bad way, you are going to find it bad. Therefore look at everything as good, and you are going to find happiness. But if you look at everything as bad, then badness is going to come, in fact, from your inner self, within you.

Today is the second day of the holy month of Rajab. The Prophet ﷺ said:

> *Rajab is the month of God, and Shaʻban is my month, and Ramadan is the month of my Community.*[114]

"Shaʻban is my month" means that God has given the Prophet ﷺ authority over all human beings during that month. No angels can write anything on you without first obtaining permission from the Prophet ﷺ. As God loved human beings and created them perfect, the Prophet ﷺ was created by God and given that authority over this Community to keep it pure and clean. The Prophet ﷺ has therefore ordered saints all over the world, to be helpers for him in cleaning and balancing the good and the bad that everyone has done, every twenty-four hours.

The Sufi secrets are not secret. They are secret only to those who have not heard them before. To others they are well known

---

[114] Abu 'l-Fath ibn Abi Fawaris in his *Amalee*, ad-Daylami, Ibn al-Jawzi, al-Hafiz Ibn Hajar in *Kitab tabayyin al-ʻajab fima warada fi rajab*.

because they are always with the Prophet ﷺ, always receiving this high knowledge from his heart.

## 12,000 Oceans of Knowledge on Each Letter of Qur'an

On every letter of the holy Qur'an God has given the Prophet ﷺ 12,000 oceans of knowledge. Do you think, however, that *alif* is a single letter in the Qur'an? If it is repeated, it is considered a new letter in every repetition. Every occurrence of every letter of the alphabet in the Qur'an, therefore, carries 12,000 oceans of knowledge with it.

All that the Prophet ﷺ has shown us of knowledge, following God's Order, is like a drop in an endless ocean. God is keeping what is left for the hearts of human beings to discover; with these physical bodies we cannot grasp that knowledge. That is why Sayyidina Abu Hurayrah ؓ could not explain everything that the Prophet ﷺ had put in his heart. Why did he say they would have cut his neck? Because they are jealous.

Scholars of different faiths are jealous of each other. They do not want all human beings to find God's mercy; they want that only for those of their own faith. God said, there is no discrimination: human beings are all servants and are therefore all at the same level—servants of God, each one of them. Following the Prophet ﷺ, we consider that all human beings in creation are the same, for Prophet Muhammad ﷺ said:

*Human beings are equal like the teeth of a comb.*[115]

And God will judge everyone, it is not up to the scholars of different faiths, but it is up to God's Divine Judgment, Who possesses absolute Divine Justice.

---

[115] Ad-Daylami from Sahl bin Sa'd.

Here is a story to illustrate this principle, told to us by our Grandshaykh, Shaykh Abdullah al-Fa'iz ad-Daghestani ق, and by our master, Shaykh Muhammad Nazim al-Haqqani ق. It is one of the hidden secrets that will be opened, with God's permission, in the time of Jesus ﷺ and Mahdi ﷺ.

## The Robe of the Prophet and Uwais al-Qarani

The Prophet ﷺ ordered Sayyidina 'Umar and Sayyidina 'Ali ؓ that, as soon as he passes away, before his burial, and after the funeral prayer, his robe should be taken to Sayyidina Uwais al-Qarani ؓ and given to him, because he was designated to keep it. He told them to give it as a trust to Uwais from himself, and to give even themselves, Sayyidina 'Umar and Sayyidina 'Ali ؓ, as trusts into the hands of Uwais. They were astonished: how were they, the best Companions, to give themselves to Uwais, and who was Uwais, who never came to see the Prophet ﷺ? Why did he never come? Because his mother had told him, "Don't leave me alone; don't go," so he didn't go.

As the Prophet ﷺ was passing away he was sweating profusely. If you look at anyone passing away, you will find them sweating. Much water comes out of their body. Of all people in this world, the Prophet ﷺ sweated most. One could easily squeeze water out of his robe at that time. It was completely soaked. Afterwards, they took his robe and went seeking Uwais, to the place the Prophet ﷺ had mentioned. There, they asked for Uwais al-Qarani ؓ whom the Prophet ﷺ had named, but no one knew such a person. Sayyidina 'Umar ؓ was becoming angry. Sayyidina 'Ali ؓ said, "O 'Umar, wait and see. Let us check the matter more closely. What the Prophet ﷺ told us, must happen, and we will find Uwais, by God's leave."

After they asked further, they finally found Sayyidina Uwais al-Qarani ؓ sitting on a rock with a stick in his hand. He was a shepherd. His mother was beside him, looking at his face. They came to him and Sayyidina 'Umar asked him, "What is your name?" He answered, "'Abd Allah."[116] Sayyidina 'Umar asked, "What is your family name?" He replied, "'Abd Allah."

"I am also 'Abd Allah," said Sayyidina 'Umar ☙, "But what is your real name?" "'Abd Allah is my real name," the man replied. Then Sayyidina 'Umar ☙ looked at Sayyidina 'Ali ☙ and told him, "We didn't find the correct person. His name is 'Abd Allah?" Sayyidina 'Ali ☙ asked the man, "O 'Abd Allah, I accept the fact that your real name is 'Abd Allah. But what do your people call you?" He answered, "Uwais al-Qarani."

Every person's real name is 'Abd Allah, servant of God. Every human being has seven names on the Preserved Tablets[117], in the Divine Presence, one of which is 'Abd Allah. This is a favor God has granted every human, to be the servant of his or her Lord.

Sayyidina 'Umar ☙ was happy. At that point and before anything else was said to him, Sayyidina Uwais al-Qarani ☙ said, "Give me the trust that the Prophet ﷺ sent me." How did he know that the Prophet ﷺ was sending him his robe when he had never met him? He took the robe and put it on his head out of respect. He looked at Sayyidina 'Umar ☙ and said, "Do you know what is in that robe?" Sayyidina 'Umar ☙ answered, "You tell me." Sayyidina Uwais al-Qarani ☙ said, "It contains the secret of all human beings. And the Prophet ﷺ is putting that responsibility on my shoulders."[xxxvi]

## God Did Not Create Humankind for Punishment

God has created this world and has not left it. He sent to this world messengers, and after them saints, to keep human beings

---

[116] lit. Servant of God.
[117] Preserved Tablet, Arabic: *al-Lawh al-Mahfudh*. A heavenly record in which God has written the destinies of all created beings, prior to their creation in this world.

clean from mistakes. God did not create us to send us to hell. He created us to put us in paradises. He created us because He loved us. Do not ever think that God created you to send you to hell and punishment. He is the Most Merciful. He created you with complete love and mercy. How does the mother love her child? A mother's love is only a drop in of God's Love Oceans. Do not, therefore, think that God seeks to punish anyone. We hope He will clean everyone and punish them before they pass from this world. And this might be done in ways we do not know of.

Sayyidina 'Umar asked, "How is the secret of human beings in this robe?" Sayyidina Uwais responded, "O 'Umar, did you ever see the Prophet ?" He answered, "What kind of question are you asking! I was with him every day!" Sayyidina Uwais said, "Describe to me his features." Sayyidina 'Umar proceeded to describe the Prophet's face, the color of his eyes, and so forth. Sayyidina Uwais said, "Ignorant people knew him in that way. Describe to me his spiritual appearance." Out of respect, Sayyidina 'Umar kept silent.

"What about you, O 'Ali?" Sayyidina Uwais asked, "Did you see the Prophet ?" He answered, "I saw the Prophet once. He called me, and told me, 'O 'Ali, look from my belly up.' I looked, and I found that everything up to his neck was under the Throne of God, but I couldn't see his neck. And he told me to look from the belly down, and I saw his knees were reaching to the seventh earth, but I couldn't see his legs. Then he told me look at him all. I looked, and I saw everything disappear except the Prophet : he was everything."

This means that if Sayyidina 'Ali could have seen where the neck of the Prophet is reaching, he would have been like the Prophet . But no can be like him, and therefore that was his limit. He couldn't see his legs: everything disappeared below the knees, which were already reaching to the seventh earth. No one knows what or where that "seventh earth" is, it is a secret. "He was everything" refers to what we were saying before concerning our creation by God from the three lights: the light of God, the light of the Prophet ﷺ, and the light of Adam ؑ, also implied in the verse of Qur'an mentioning God's honoring human beings.[118] How God honored human beings is a secret; but from that secret we can understand that God has honored us by creating us from these three lights.

If human beings are created from these three lights, how can they be dirtied? Never. Nothing can sully the light of God; nor the light of the Prophet ﷺ; nor the light of our father Adam ؑ. We are created from these three lights and these three lights can never be polluted. This is why everyone has the name "Servant of God," 'Abd Allah," in the Divine Presence.

Sayyidina Uwais told Sayyidina 'Ali ؓ, "O 'Ali, you saw the Prophet ﷺ one time." Sayyidina 'Ali ؓ asked him, "Have you seen the Prophet?" He answered, "Physically, I have never seen him in all my life. Spiritually, I was with the Prophet ﷺ always, without interruption, twenty-four hours a day."[xxxvii]

Sayyidina 'Umar ؓ cried and said, "This explains to me the importance of 'Ali in my life, and the importance of the hadith of the Prophet ﷺ:

*I am the city of knowledge, and 'Ali is the door.*[119]

This month of Rajab will not finish before all sincere ones on earth are cleaned from their sins and light is put in their hearts. The power that God gave to the Prophet ﷺ to cleanse hearts, He also gave to saints. Saints are helpers for the Prophet ﷺ in this month. That is why saints are continually busy in Rajab. They don't speak with anyone. They like to shut their doors and sit in

---

[118] *Verily We have honored the Children of Adam* (Suratu 'l-Isra, 17:70).
[119] At-Tirmidhi. Hakim, Ibn 'Asakir, al-'Iraqi, al-Haythami, as-Suyuti.

their rooms, not going out, because they are constantly asking their Lord forgiveness for human beings.

## The Dowry of Fatimah

The daughter of the Prophet ﷺ, Our Lady Fatimah al-Zahra ؇, when she saw that her father was constantly saying, "O my Lord! My Community," she also wanted to do something for the benefit of this Community. Look and see how hard saints are trying to save human beings and prevent them from falling into sins and mistakes. When God ordered the Prophet ﷺ to marry his daughter to someone, the Prophet ﷺ called all Companions ؇ without discrimination and said to them, "God has ordered me tonight to say that anyone who reads Qur'an from beginning to end tonight will marry my daughter Fatimah."

That night, all Companions ؇ were trying to read the Holy Qur'an from beginning to end. All stayed at the mosque trying to finish it, except Sayyidina 'Ali ؇ who went home and slept.

When Bilal made the call for the pre-dawn prayer, all came to the mosque and the Prophet ﷺ was present. After finishing the prayer, Prophet Muhammad ﷺ asked, "Who finished the Qur'an last night, so that I will marry him to my daughter Fatimah?" No one was able to answer, because it is very difficult to finish the thirty parts (*juz'*) in only seven or eight hours. Sayyidina 'Ali ؇ said, "O Messenger of God, I finished reading Qur'an last night." The others looked at him with jealousy saying, "How is it that you completed the Qur'an? You were in bed sleeping the whole night." He said, "No, I completed Qur'an from beginning to end." The Prophet ﷺ said to Sayyidina 'Ali ؇, "Who is your witness?" Sayyidina 'Ali ؇ said, "God is my witness and you, O Prophet, are my witness that I completed it."

Now listen carefully, for Mawlana Shaykh Nazim emphasized this point. The Prophet ﷺ—as you know—never tried to show that he knew of something happening outside his normal scope before

Archangel Gabriel ﷺ informed him. He waited, therefore, for inspiration to come. The angel Archangel Gabriel ﷺ descended and told him, "God is informing you that 'Ali is telling the truth and that he has completed the Qur'an tonight. So ask him what he has done."

The Prophet ﷺ said to the Companions ؓ, "The angel Gabriel ﷺ has just now come to me and told me that 'Ali ؓ has completed the Qur'an and God is his witness. I am therefore his witness also, and I am asking 'Ali ؓ what he has read last night."

Sayyidina 'Ali ؓ said, "O Messenger of God, I read *Ashhadu an La ilaha illa-Allah wa ashhadu anna Muhammadur-Rasulullah* three times, then *Astaghfirullah* seventy times, then the Opening Chapter of Qur'an (al-Fatihah) once, then the Chapter of Sincerity (al-Ikhlas) three times, then the Chapter of the Daybreak (al-Falaq) one time, then the Chapter of Mankind (an-Nas) one time, then ten times *La ilaha illa-Allah*, ten times *Allahumma salli 'ala Muhammadin wa 'ala Ali Muhammadin wa sallim*."

The Prophet ﷺ said, "As God has witnessed that 'Ali has completed the Qur'an, I am witnessing as well, that if you read what we just described, you are completing the Qur'an." At that time the hadith was related making three readings of Surat al-Ikhlas (*Qul Huwa Allahu Ahad*...) equivalent to reading the whole Qur'an.[xxxviii]

Reading this every day will hardly take two minutes of your time: but it is as if you read the whole Qur'an. Ignorant people sit trying to read and complete the Qur'an with pride and they cannot finish. You can do this small reading and finish, and it is as if you had completed the Qur'an. What more do you want? And thus was Fatimah ؓ married to 'Ali.

Look at Fatimah's ؓ marriage and do not say that ladies enjoy no freedom in Islam. You would be mistaken. God has given freedom and equality between men and women. They can give their own opinions and take their own decisions. Even the Prophet ﷺ asked his daughter, and said to the Companions ؓ, "I have to ask my daughter whether she accepts this marriage or not; it is her decision."

## Islam Honors Ladies

Ignorant people say nowadays that Islam did not give rights to ladies. This is what they say but do not have to believe them. We believe what we read and hear from the Prophet ﷺ. He gave equality as God gave equality. Ladies have the same rights as men. This is what we believe, and Americans especially have to beware of saying "Islam gave no rights to ladies."

The Prophet ﷺ asked Fatimah ؓ, "O Fatimah, do you accept 'Ali as your husband?" She said, "No." All the Companions ؓ were looking at Sayyidina 'Ali ؓ, at Fatimah ؓ, at the Prophet ﷺ. The Prophet ﷺ felt red in the face: why is Fatimah ؓ saying no? Was she in love with someone else? The Prophet ﷺ did not know what to say, and the Archangel Gabriel ؑ came and told him, "O Messenger of God, do not take a hasty decision concerning her. God is telling you to ask her why she is not accepting." The Prophet ﷺ turned to Our Lady Fatimah ؓ and said, "O Fatimah, you said 'no.' Never mind, this is your decision. But can I know why you are not accepting?" She said, "I only said 'no' because I am accept, but only on one condition. It does not concern 'Ali, but it is related to me. If you accept that condition from me, I will accept. If not, I will never accept to marry 'Ali." Again, the angel Gabriel ؑ came to the Prophet ﷺ saying, "God is ordering you to ask her what her condition is." Now look what God had put in her heart—then consider the benefit and station of ladies in Islam.

The Prophet ﷺ said, "O Fatimah, what is your condition?" She said, "It is very easy. If God accepts and you, my father, accept, I accept. If God does not accept, I do not accept to marry. When you came to this world, you were saying, 'My Community, my

Community—*Ummatee, ummatee!*' and in your life, day and night, I hear you in the house always asking, 'My Community, O my Lord! Give me leave to lead my Community to You! Forgive them! Purify them! Take away their sins and burdens and difficulties!' I hear you, and know how much you are suffering for your Community. And I know from what you said, that when you pass away you will still be saying, 'My Community! *Ummatee!*' before your Lord, in your grave, and on Judgment Day."

"My Community," means all human beings, and the Prophet ﷺ came for every human being—not only for Muslims. It is a big mistake to interpret "My Community" in that restricted, limited sense. The Prophet ﷺ came for everyone. Allah said:

> *Say (O Muhammad), "O humankind! I am sent unto ye all, as the Messenger of God..."* [120]

There were no Muslims at that time and the Prophet ﷺ came for all the people at that time: Christians, Jews, and the pagans of the Era of Ignorance (*Jahiliyyah*). Those that believed in him are called Muslims: they are known as the Community that Responded (*Ummatu 'l-Ijaba*). Those who did not believe him are known as the Community of the Message (*Ummatu 'd-Da'wah*): they are on the outer fringe; but it remains that the Prophet ﷺ came for them, and they are therefore his Community.

Fatimah ؏ continued, "Since I see you, my father, suffering so much for your Community, and since that love of your Community is also in my heart, I want your Community as my dowry. If you accept, I will marry 'Ali." She asked for all of the Prophet's Community—everyone, without discrimination. "I want them as my dowry in order to have that dowry in my hand when I rise on Judgment Day, and receive that dowry from my

---

[120] Suratu 'l-'Araf, 7:158.

Lord, to enter them into my Paradise. If you don't accept, I will not marry 'Ali."

What was the Prophet ﷺ going to say? It was not in his hand to give such a dowry. He waited for Archangel Gabriel ؏, but Archangel Gabriel ؏ did not come quickly. He kept him waiting some time. When he finally came he said, "God is sending you His greetings of peace, and is accepting Fatimah's request, and is giving her all of the Community as her dowry to marry 'Ali." Immediately, the Prophet ﷺ stood up and made two cycles of the Prayer of Thanks (*shukr*) in thanks to his Lord.

Lady Fatimah ؇ did not say, "I want money or jewelry" as the ladies of today, or as men trying to marry rich ladies. She was only looking out for the Community of the Prophet ﷺ. Not one of this Community is going to be outside of her dowry, because if God removes one person from the dowry, it will be as if she had lived with Sayyidina 'Ali in wrongdoing. Therefore, she is going to take all the Community under her wing and they shall enter with her into Paradise.

This is from the power of one spiritually-attained lady. She is taking everyone with her into Paradise. Do you think anyone will be left outside? Because of her, no one will be left outside. What about the many such ladies in Islam? What will be their power? What about saints? What about prophets? That is why God has created human beings clean, and He is keeping them clean with such power as that of Lady Fatimah ؇, Sayyidina 'Ali ؇, Sayyidina 'Umar ؇, the Prophet ﷺ, our Grandshaykh, our Shaykh Mawlana Shaykh Nazim, the masters of the Naqshbandi order—all working to keep everyone clean and pure.

Be happy therefore, be satisfied with the conditions in which God has created you. When you are satisfied and happy, you are going to find happiness and satisfaction all your life.

# APPENDIX

## Invocation of Rajab

Bismillāhi 'r-Raḥmāni 'r-Raḥīm.
Allāhumma innī astaghfiruka min kulli mā tubtu 'anhu ilayka thumma 'udtu fīhi. Wa astaghfiruka min kulli mā āradtu bihi wajhaka fakhālaṭani fīhi la laysa fīhi raḍā'uk. Wa astaghfiruka li 'n-ni'am 'illatī taqawwaytu bihā 'alā m'aṣīyatik. Wa astaghfiruka min adh-dhunūb 'illati lā y'alamuhā ghayruka, wa lā yaṭali'u 'alayhā aḥadun siwāk wa lā tasa'ūhā illa raḥmatika, wa lā tunjī minhā illa maghfiratuka wa ḥilmuka. Lā ilāha illa Anta subḥānaka innī kuntu mina 'ẓ-ẓālimīn.

In the name of God, the Merciful, the Compassionate
O Allah, I ask forgiveness of You for everything for which I repented to You then returned to. And I ask forgiveness of You for everything I displeased You with and all that concerns me with which You are displeased. And I ask forgiveness of You for the favors which I used for increasing my disobedience towards You. And I ask forgiveness of You for the sins which no one knows except You and no one sees except You and nothing encompasses except Your Mercy and nothing delivers from except Your forgiveness and clemency. There is no god except You alone. Glory be to You! Indeed I was an oppressor to myself.

Allāhuma innī istaghfiruka min kulli ẓulmin ẓalamtu bihi 'ibādak. Fa ayyumā 'abdin min 'ibādika aw amatin min imā'ika ẓalamtu fī badanihi aw 'irḍihi aw mālihi fa-ā'atihi min khazā'iniki 'llatī lā tanquṣ. Wa as'aluka an tukrimanī bi-raḥmatiki 'llatī wasi'at kulla shay'in wa lā tuhīnanī bi-'adhābika wa tu'ṭīyyanī mā as'aluka fa-innī ḥaqīqun bi-raḥmatika ya arḥamu 'r-Rāhimīn. Wa ṣalla-Allāhu 'alā Sayyidinā Muḥammadin wa 'alā ālihi wa ṣāḥbihi ajm'aīn. Wa lā ḥawla wa lā quwatta illa

O Allah, I ask forgiveness of You for the injustice I committed against Your servants. Whatever of Your male or female servants whom I have hurt, physically or in their dignity or in their property, give them of Your bounty which lacks nothing. And I ask You to honor me with Your mercy which encompasses all things. Do not humble me with Your punishment but give me what I ask of You, for I am in great need of Your mercy, O Most billāhi 'l-ʿAliyyi 'l-ʿAẓīm.

Merciful of the merciful. May Allah send blessings upon Muhammad and upon all his Companions. There is no power and no strength save in God, the Most High, the Great.

# ENDNOTES

[i] Prophet Muhammad ﷺ said:
   If there was just one day left in the world, God would extend that day so He would send a man from my family whose name and whose father's name are the same as mine. He will fill the earth with equity and justice just as it was filled with oppression and tyranny. (Abu Dawud reported it from Ibn Mas'ud in his *Sunan*)

Abu Hurayrah ؓ related that Muhammad, the Messenger of God ﷺ said:
   Jesus the son of Mary ؑ will come as a just ruler and a just leader. (Al-Mutaqqi)

[ii] Sultan al-Awliya Shaykh 'Abd Allah ad-Daghestani ق said:
   Seclusion and isolation is an emphatic practice (*as-sunnah al-mu'akkadah*) among the ways of the practice, especially for the master of the Prophets, Muhammad ﷺ. For the saints it is an obligatory practice especially for the major shaykhs of the distinguished Naqshbandi Way. Where the Imam of the Way, Shah Naqshband ق said, "Each of you should be ashamed to claim relationship to the most distinguished Naqshbandi Way if he has not once completed forty days of seclusion."

   Grandshaykh 'Abd Allah taught that before any major form of worship, the seeker should repeat, "I intend forty (days), I intend seclusion in the mosque, I intend seclusion, I intend isolation, I intend (spiritual) discipline, I intend to travel in the Path for the sake of God in this gathering." He should say this at the time of prayer of the obligatory and implicated prayers or when reading the Qur'an or *Dala'il al-Khayrat*. Also when he sits to complete his devotions and the litanies every day or night and when he attends the Circle of the Masters, prays in congregation or any type of worship whatsoever.

   The benefit of this intention is that it is counted by God from the time you begin until you complete the worship, until it corresponds to the number of days for seclusion and it is written for you as if you completed a complete seclusion in the most distinguished Naqshbandi Way.

[iii] The Prophet ﷺ said:

> The most beloved servants to God are those who endear God to his servants and endear his servants to Him. And they walk the earth giving sincere advice. (an-Naysaburi reports it in a different wording from Abu Dharr, Ibn Mubarak also related it with a different chain.)

After citing this hadith in his *Revival of the Religious Sciences*, in the chapter "Exposition of the Rank of Shaykhhood," Imam al-Ghazali ق (1058-1111) said:

> This is the rank of Shaykhhood and calling to God that the Messenger of God ﷺ mentioned. Because the shaykh literally endears God to his servants and endears the servants to God. The rank of Shaykhhood is among the highest ranks in the path of Sufism and it is the representation of Prophethood in calling to God...because the shaykh places the seeker on the path of emulating the Messenger of God ﷺ. And the one who has perfected his emulation of him ﷺ and follows him, then God loves him...

[iv] God says:

> ***Cling to the rope of God and do not separate.*** (Surat Ali-'Imran, 3:103)

And God's Messenger ﷺ said: The most beloved to God are those who make harmony and those who are well-acqainted. (at-Tabarani in his *al-Awsat* and his *as-Saghir* from Abu Hurayra ؓ.)

And Prophet Muhammad ﷺ related that God said:

> My love is incumbent for those who love one another for My sake, who assemble for My sake and those who visit each other for My sake. (*hadith qudsi* narrated from Mu'adh as reported by Ahmad in his *Musnad*, at-Tabarani in his *Kabir*, al-Hakim in his *Mustadrak* and al-Bayhaqi in his *Shu'b*).

[v] Ibn 'Abbas ؓ said of the verse: ***Whoever forgives and makes peace takes his reward from God*** (Ash-Shura, 42:40):

The one who does not retaliate [for injury] and patches up what is between him and the oppressor by forgiveness, *his reward is with God;* God [Himself] will reward him for that. (Imam al-Qurtubi related it in his commentary of the Holy Qur'an)

Ibn 'Abbas related:

On the Day of Judgment a caller will summon those who have something deserving God's reward. It would be said to them, "What have you done?" They will say, "We forgave those who oppressed us." And that is the Word of God, **"Whoever forgives and makes peace takes his reward from God."** It would be said to them, "Enter Paradise by the permission of God." (Al-Hafiz as-Suyuti in his *Tafsir*)

In his *Tafsir* At-Tabari said:

This verse is for the one one who forgives the one who wronged him and did not chastise him. The reward for his forgiveness is with God. And God is Grantor of his reward.

vi Regarding the verse: **Surely a happy state shall be attained by the believers** (Suratu 'l-Muminoon, 23:1), K'ab said:

God didn't create anything with His Hands except three: He created Adam with His hands, He created the Torah with His Hands and He planted the Garden of Eden with His Hands. Then God said to the garden, "speak," and it said, *"surely a happy state shall attain to the believers,"* when it understood the blessing it contained. (Al-Hafiz as-Suyuti recorded it in his commentary from 'Abd-Razzaq and Ibn Jarir)

Ishaq bin Rahuway said, "It is true that God created Adam in the picture of The Merciful." (Al-Asqalani in his *Fath* from Harb al-Karmani's *Kitab as-Sunnah*. Ishaq al-Khawsaj said he heard that Ahmad said it is authentic.)

Al-Manawi in *Fayd al-Qadir*, the commentary of al-Hafiz as-Suyuti's *Jami'*, explains this hadith:

He created Adam in a fashion that He loved from Himself He made it from all His creation. Because there is nothing in existence except that it has a likeness in His Image. That is why it is said that man is a microcosm.

He relates that Ibn 'Arabi ق (1165-1240) said:

When it came the time in God's knowledge to fashion the Vicegerent, by whom God guides the angels by means of his existence, and this was a period of seven thousand years, He commanded the angels to bring Him a handful of every type of soil from the earth and they brought it to Him. God took it and fermented it with His Hands...

[vii] Abu Hurayrah ؓ related from the Prophet ﷺ, "God does not look at your forms and wealth, rather He looks at your hearts and your actions." (Muslim)

'Ali ؓ said, "Adam ؑ was created from the surface of the earth wherein is a pleasant scent, virtue and vice. And all of this is what you see in his progeny." (Al-Hafiz as-Suyuti)

Abi Dharr ؓ related that he heard the Prophet ﷺ say, "Adam was created from three types of soils; black, white and red." (Ibn 'Asakir and Ibn S'ad)

[viii] Abu Sa'id al-Khudri ؓ related that the Messenger of God ﷺ said:

Beware of the vision of the believer, because he sees with the light of God. (Tirmidhi)

Ibn 'Umar ؓ and Thawban ؓ narrated this tradition with the added words at the end, "...and he speaks in correspondence with God." (Ibn Jarir)

[ix] Ibn 'Abbas ؓ said:

Knowledge is the life of Islam and the pillar of belief. Who learns some knowledge will be rewarded by God. But the one who learns, then acts upon his knowledge, God will teach what he did not know before. (Abu ash-Shaykh)

[x] Abu Hurayrah ؓ related from the Messenger of God ﷺ that God says:

I am as My servant thinks of Me. And I am with him when he mentions Me. If he mentions Me to himself, I mention him to Myself. And if he mentions Me in a gathering, I mention him in the company of those who are in My Presence. (Bukhari and Muslim)

[xi] God says in the Qur'an: *Say! We believe in God and what He hath sent to us and what hath He sent to Abraham, Ishmael, Isaac, Jacob and the tribes. And what was given to Moses and Jesus and the*

*prophets from their Lord. We make no distinction between them and we are the ones who submit to God.* (Surat Ali-'Imran, 3:84).

[xii] God says: *The servants of the Merciful are those who walk upon the earth in tranquility. And when they are met by the ignorant, they say "peace."* (Suratu 'l-Furqan, 25:63).

Malik bin Anas ؓ reported that the Messenger of God ﷺ said:

> O my son, if you are able to meet the Lord morning and evening without hatred in your heart for anyone, then do so. (Al-Hafiz as-Suyuti from at-Tirmidhi in his *Ziyadah*)

[xiii] 'Uthman ؓ related from the Prophet ﷺ:

> He who dies and knows there is no deity except God, shall enter paradise. (Bukhari)

Abu Dharr ؓ reported that the Prophet ﷺ said:

> Who bears witness that there is no diety except God, shall enter Paradise; even if he commits adultery and steals. (Al-Hindi in his *Kanz* and Ahmad in his *Musnad*)

[xiv] Cf. Surah Ya Sin, 36:9. Prophet Muhammad ﷺ recited this verse as he stepped out from his home in Makkah (migrating to the city of Madinah), when it was surrounded by those of his townspeople who sought to capture and kill him. By means of it he was able to pass unnoticed by them after they fell asleep outside his home.

[xv] C.f. Suratu 'l-Fil, 105:1 5. Abraha was a Yemeni king who built a huge cathedral and hoped all people would make pilgrimage to it. However he came to hear about the Ka'bah and the annual pilgrimage there. Out of jealousy, he assembled a large army, and accompanied by thirteen battle elephants, proceeded to Makkah. When he reached there the Prophet's grandfather, 'Abd al-Muttalib, leader of the tribes in Makkah, advised his people to leave the city, saying "The Lord of the House well able to protect it." As the army neared Makkah, God sent forth an army composed of birds, carrying heated stones of baked clay with which they pelted Abraha and his army, decimating them. This occurred in the year of Prophet Muhammad's ﷺ birth (570 CE), known also as "Year of the Elephant."

[xvi] Ibn Mas'ud related from the Prophet ﷺ:

> Among the signs and conditions of the Hour, is that the traitor would be trusted while the trustworthy one would be accused of

treachery; the liar would be believed and the truthful one rejected. (At-Tabarani in his *Awsat* and *Kabir*, al-Qastalani in his *Majmu'* and al-Hindi in his *Kanz*)

xvii Abu Sa'id related that the Prophet ﷺ said:
Never do a people sit remembering God except that the angels will surround them and they will be enveloped with mercy, tranquility will descend upon them, and God will mention them among those who are in His Presence. (Muslim and Tirmidhi)

Anas ؓ related that the Prophet ﷺ said:
God has roving angels who search out the circles of God's remembrance. When they find them they cover them with their wings and God says, "Cover them with My mercy for they are a group for whom there is no distress." (Al-Bazzar)

xviii While this saying is not raised to the status of hadith, according to the scholars of traditions (*muhaddithin*) the meaning is true, based on the hadith of Ibn 'Abbas ؓ from ad-Daruqtni's *Afrad*, "Among the acts of humility is the one who drinks the remains of his brother."

Al-'Ajluni said, "I was sitting with sermoners of Damascus in a gathering. A cup bearer approached to quench our thirst, and I withheld from drinking [from the common cup]. And the preacher said to me, 'the saliva of a believer is a healing.'"

xix According to the People of Reality, *Ahl al-Haqq*, heavenly knowledge, (*'ilmun ladunni*), is of three types:

a. Revelation (*wahiyy*); a communication only between God and his chosen Prophets.

b. Inspiration (*ilham*); a type of Prophetic dream inspired by God to divine personalities for the benefit of mankind.

c. Stage of Vision (*Darajat al-firasat*); a stage of the highly developed divine intelligence acquired by saints and the pious.

d. Unveiling (*Kashf*); the hidden or secret knowledge both of earthly or heavenly things. This knowledge also lies dormant and hidden in certain verses of the Holy Quran. This knowledge is interpreted by those Sufis only who reach the pinnacle of spirituality.

xx The People of Reality (*Ahl al-Haqq*) describe the attainment of knowledge according to these criteria:

The Scholars of Outer Knowledge (*'ulama al-dhahir*):
Pertains to knowledge which can be gained by means of study and intelligence and is received from schools and universities. At this stage the carnal soul has not given up disobedience. Belief and worship are in a superficial form because the ego has yet to become a [true] believer.

The Scholars of Inner Knowledge (*'ulama al-batin*):
Knowledge attained through divine inspiration which pertains to one's spiritual state and purity. At this stage the carnal soul has perished.

One who is imparted directly from God without the medium of schools, etc. This is known as the secret or hidden knowledge. At this stage the soul attains firm belief and faith is protected; at this stage one's worship is real.

xxi Describing an event that took place on the night of Ascension the Holy Prophet ﷺ said:
My Lord revealed to me three different types of knowledge. He told me not to reveal the first to anyone because none but I can understand it. He said, "You may communicate the second science to whom you wish and teach the third to all of your Community."
(Al-Qastalani in *al-Mawahib*)

xxii Ibn 'Umar ؓ relates:
Take account of yourselves before you are taken to account. Weigh yourselves before you are weighed because it will be less for you in the weighing of tomorrow (Day of Judgment). Prepare yourself for the greatest event, **On that day you will be shown your deeds and nothing will be hidden.** (Suratu 'l-Haqqah, 69:18). (Ibn Mubarak, Ahmad in his *Zuhd* and Ibn Abi Dunya in his *Muhasabah*)

xxiii Al-Hajj 'Umar al-Futi ق (1797-1864) said in his *Rimah*, "By association with the elite, one obtains three traits:
the acquisition of knowledge
purity of the heart and
a peaceful state."

xxiv Imam Ahmad narrated that the fast of 'Ashura, "atones the sins of two years, the preceding year and the coming year."

xxv Abu Sa'id al-Khudri ﷺ related that the Messenger of God ﷺ said:
> The Mahdi ﷺ will be with my Community for seven, eight or nine years. My Community will experience a delight like no other has enjoyed before. The skies will give rain in abundance and the earth will withhold nothing of its vegetation. Wealth will be in stacks and a man will say, "O Mahdi, give me some of it." He will says, "Take as much as you like." (Al-Hafiz, Abu Nu'aym and at-Tabarani)

xxvi This is because spiritual vision, as explained above, is the lowest form of unveiling. Because according to the teachings of the renowned Moroccan saint 'Abd al-'Aziz ad-Dabbagh ق (d. 1719), unveiling (*kashf*) has two degrees :

> God created truth and light and He created people for it. And He also created darkness and falsehood and people for it. For them darkness is open as is the knowledge of whatever is connected to it. But for the people of reality and truth (*Haqq*), is the opening of truth and reality, its knowledge and whatever is related to it. The truth, is to believe in God and the establishment of His Lordship, to believe that He creates whatever He will, and to believe in the angels.
>
> Darkness is attachment to everything that severs one from God such as the worldly life, its fleeting matters and events. Sufficient for you is the the Prophet's ﷺ saying, "The world and whatever is in it are cursed except the remembrance of God and what relates to it."
>
> Reality is among the lights from God that He showers on the people of truth. But God showers on the people of falsehood darkness, so that their intellects are darkened and their vision is blinded from the truth... For the people of truth, there is the opening in the first degree and in the second degree.
>
> The first degree is everything that is opened for the people of darkness in the heavens and the earth, such as the knowledge of the constellations. He sees the levels of the earth and the heavens and whatever is in them and he sees what people do in their homes and palaces. He does not see this with his eyes, but he sees this with his inner vision that no barrier obstructs nor walls repel.

And he sees the future, such as what is going to happen in a certain month or year. For both they and the people of darkness are granted this portion of success. This is the reason why it is said that unveiling is the weakest of the stage of sainthood (*wilayah*) in that it is found with the people of truth and with the people of darkness. And its possessor is not safe from his ego being cut off from God and adhering to the people of darkness (as happened to some Sufis).

As far as the second level of opening, what is opened to him is the witnessing of the secrets of reality which are veiled from the people of darkness. They see the saints of God, speak with them and receive their assistance, even from a vast distance. He sees the souls of the believers above their graves, the noble recording angels and the other angels. He sees the isthmus (between the worldly life and the afterlife) and the souls therein. And he sees the resting place (*qabr*) of the Prophet ﷺ and the rays of light extending from it to the dome of the Isthmus. When he attains the vision of the person (*dhat*) of the Prophet ﷺ in wakefulness, he has attained safety from the traps of Satan because of his connection with the Mercy of God, (as manifest) in our leader, our Prophet, our master, Muhammad ﷺ.

xxvii Al-Hajj 'Umar al-Futi ق gave a stern warning in his *Rimah Hizb ar-Rahim*, about one who claims Shaykhhood based solely on his actions:

Some of the shaykhs say, "He who desires to be a shaykh without it being a matter from God, is an imbecile. And who desires to be a shaykh without it being a grant from God, is insane. And he who desires to be a shaykh by his own endeavor is ignorant...and he who desires to be a shaykh for the pleasure and a station with creation, is a hypocrite."

xxviii Sayyidina 'Umar ؓ reported that the Messenger of God ﷺ said, "Actions are according to intentions." (Bukhari, at-Tirmidhi, Abu Dawud and many others)

xxix "I am raising you from the level of imitation, which is the common level for everyone, to the level of seeing" is an allusion to the journey of the Sufi, as in the explanation Imam Ghazali ق gives of the hadith in which a Bedouin asked the Prophet ﷺ, "when is the Hour of Judgment?"

The Prophet ﷺ replied, "And what have you prepared for it?" He said, "Nothing of many prayers nor fasting, but I do love God and His Messenger." He ﷺ said, "You will be with the one you love." (Bukhari and Muslim)

Explaining this, Imam Ghazali ق says:

> The journey of the Sufi is first through belief, then through knowledge, then through taste. The emulator (*al-mutashabbih*) is the one with belief, the aspirant is the one with knowledge and the Sufi is the one possessing taste. Belief in the way is a strong foundation. Hence Imam al-Junayd ق said, "Belief in our way is an authority."

A Sufi adept related:

> A person came to Shaykh Ahmad al-Ghazali ق [brother of Imam Ghazali ق and a renowned Sufi master] while we were in Isfahan seeking to wear the cloak [enter the Sufi Path]. So my shaykh said to that person, "Go to so-and-so," indicating myself, "to teach you the meaning of the cloak," and brought a cloak for him to wear. Then I came to him and taught him the rights due the cloak, what is obligatory in its care, the conduct of wearing it and who is fit to wear it. He was overwhelmed by the rights due the cloak and recoiled from donning it.
>
> The shaykh was informed of what had happened to the student, so he summoned me and admonished me for what I had said to him. The shaykh said, "I sent you to him in order for you to teach him in a way that you increase his ambition to don the cloak. But you taught him what reduced his determination! Though all you mentioned regarding the rights due the cloak was true, but when we impose that on the beginner he flees and is incapable of achieving it. We dress him in the cloak so that he might emulate the Folk [the Sufis] and take them as his model. This will draw him to their assemblies. The blessings of his companionship with them is that, due to his witnessing their states, he loves to travel in their ways, and he will attain something of their states."
>
> Ja'far said, "I heard Abu al-Qasim al-Junayd ق say, 'When you meet an initiate (*mubtadi'*), don't start him out with knowledge (in rules and regulations of the way); rather with leniency.

Knowledge alienates him while leniency puts him at ease. Thus, the leniency of the Sufis with the novice emulators, benefits them. All of those who have attained the best of states and were more abundant in knowledge, were most lenient with their initiates.'"

ˣˣˣ Jabir Ibn 'Abdillah reported Allah's Messenger ﷺ having said, "There would be a Caliph in the last (period) of my Ummah who would freely give handfuls of wealth to the people without counting it."... (he would be Imam Mahdi). (Muslim)

Abu Sa'id al-Khudri ؓ narrated that Prophet ﷺ said:

> Severe calamity from the direction of their ruler will befall my people during the Last Days. It will be a calamity which, in severity, shall be unprecedented. It will be so violent that the earth with injustice and corruption will shrivel for its inhabitants. The believers will not find refuge from oppression. At that time God will send a man from my family to fill the earth with justice and equity just as it is filled with injustice and tyranny. The dwellers of the heavens and the earth will be pleased with him. The earth will bring forth all that grows for him, and the heavens will pour down rains in abundance. He will live among the people for seven or nine years. From all the good that God will bestow on the inhabitants of the earth, the dead will wish to come to life again. (Ibn Hajar in *al-Sawa'iq al muhriqqa*, and *Yanabi' al-mawadda*)

As-Sayyid Jawad ash-Shahudi reported from Ja'far as-Sadiq ؑ:

> During the time of the Mahdi, humankind will be given rain in the month of Jamada and ten days of Rajab. Such a rain none has seen like it before. Then God will grow from it the flesh and bodies of the believers in their graves. It is though I am seeing them shaking off the dust of their hairs.

Ash-Shahūdī added:

> It will rain in the month of Jamadah and Rajab and after this God will revive the flesh and bodies of the believers in their graves. Abu 'Abd Allāh ؑ said, "When the Mahdi comes, an angel will come to the grave of a believer and say to him, 'O dweller of the grave, your companion (al-Mahdi ؑ) has appeared. If you wish to join him, then do so. If you wish to remain in the bliss of your

Lord (in the grave), then remain (there in the grave)." (*Al-Imam al-Mahdi and His Appearance*)

xxxi While one of the strictest scholars, Ibn Taymiyya, considered these reports false, this is narrated in *Ghazawat al-Imam ʿAli*, which says that he fought the Jinn until he sent them down to the seventh earth.

xxxii The Prophet ﷺ said, "Verily my Community is bestowed with mercy; in the afterlife there is no punishment for it...." (*Musnad* Ahmad)

xxxiii C.f.: **When Moses came to the place appointed by Us, and his Lord addressed him, He said: "O my Lord! show (Thyself) to me, that I may look upon thee." God said: "By no means canst thou see Me (direct); But look upon the mount; if it abide in its place, then shalt thou see Me." When his Lord manifested His glory on the Mount, He made it as dust. And Moses fell down in a swoon. When he recovered his senses he said: "Glory be to Thee! to Thee I turn in repentance, and I am the first of the believers."** (Suratu 'l-ʿAraf, 7:143)

xxxiv Sayyida ʿAyesha ؓ said, "Anyone wants to hear the gurgling of Kawthar, put their fingers in their ears [and they will hear it]." (*Ruh al-Bayan*)

xxxv About *fana*, a Sufi term literally signifying extinction or self-effacement, and the ecstatic utterances of some Sufis (*shatahat*) uttered in that state, Ibn Taymiyya, founder of the "Salafi" school in the 7th Hijri century, says:

> This state of love characterized many of the People of Seeking and Love of God (*Ahl al-irada*). A person vanishes to himself in the object of his love, God, through the intensity of his love. He will recall God, not recalling himself; remember God, and forget himself; take God as witness, and not take himself as witness; exist in God, not in himself. When he reaches that stage, he no longer perceives his own existence. That is why he may say in this state [as Bayazid did], "I am the Truth (*ana al-haqq*)", or, "Glory to Me! (*subhanee*)," and, "There is nothing in this cloak except God (*ma fee al-jubba illa Allah*)," because he is intoxicated with the love of God and this is a pleasure and happiness that he cannot control...
>
> ...when through his fervor, someone enters a state of ecstatic love (*ʿishq*) for God, he will take leave of his mind, and when he enters that state of absentmindedness, he will find himself as if he is

accepting the concept of union with God (*ittihad*). I do not consider this a sin, because that person is excused …as he is not aware of what he is doing. The pen does not condemn the crazed person except when he is restored to sanity (and commits the same act). However, when he is in that state and commits wrong, he will come under God's address, "***O Our Lord, do not take us to task if we forget or make mistakes,***" (Suratu 'l-Baqara, 2:286) and there is no blame on you if you unintentionally make a mistake.

xxxvi C.f. the hadith beginning: "O Muhammad. A man in your Ummah is coming who will intercede, and God will make him an intercessor." (Rawyani. Abu Nu'aym, Ibn 'Asakir, Suyuti, Haythami and others.)

xxxvii The Prophet ﷺ said:

Uwais ibn 'Amir will dawn upon you with the assistance (*imdad*) of the people of Yemen from the tribe of Murad and Qaran. He was a leper and was healed except in a tiny spot. He has a mother whose rights he keeps scrupulously. If he took an oath by God, God would fulfill it. If you are able to let him ask forgiveness for you, do it."

And:

More people will enter Paradise through the intercession of a certain man from my Community than there are people in the tribes of Rabi'a and Mudar.

Al-Hasan al-Basri said, "That is Uwais al-Qarani." (Ahmad, *al-Zuhd*) A long narration from Usair bin Jabir, concludes, "His clothing consisted of a mantle, and whosoever saw him said, 'From where did Uwais get this mantle?'" (Muslim)

xxxviii Abu 'd-Darda reported God's Messenger ﷺ as saying, "Is any of you capable of reciting a third of the Qur'an in a night?" On being asked how they could recite a third of the Qur'an he replied, "***'Say, He is God, One'*** is equivalent to a third of the Qur'an." (Bukhari and Muslim)

www.ingramcontent.com/pod-product-compliance
Lightning Source LLC
Chambersburg PA
CBHW030318080526
44584CB00012B/611